AF654976

# Preface

Planning is absolutely key if you hope to deliver inspiring lessons that both motivate and engage your students. A lesson plan is the instructor's road map of what students need to learn and how it will be done effectively during the class time.

Effective lesson planning is essential to the process of teaching and learning. Before you plan your lesson, you will first need to identify the learning objectives for the class meeting. Effective lesson preparation to ensure student learning is part of a cyclical process of planning, doing and evaluations link 'backwards' and forwards' throughout the planning process.

A successful lesson plan addresses and integrates these three key components:

- Objectives for student learning
- Teaching/learning activities
- Strategies to check student understanding

Specifying concrete objectives for student learning will help you to determine the kinds of teaching and learning activities you will use in class, while those activities will define how you will check whether the learning objectives have been accomplished.

The aim of this book is to help you, as a teacher, to further understand the principles of effective lesson planning. This will involve developing your knowledge of what promotes student learning,

In this book, best and interesting lesson plans are prepared which will be helpful to develop a different type of confidence in pupil-teacher.

We wish you a successful and rewarding career with us. Feedback in this regard is solicited.

## *Acknowledgement*

My compliments go to the **GullyBaba Publishing House (P) Ltd.,** and its meticulous team who have been enthusiastically working towards the perfection of the book.

Their teamwork, initiative and research have been very encouraging. Had it not been for their unflagging support, this work wouldn't have been possible. The creative freedom provided by them along with their aim of presenting the best to the reader has been a major source of inspiration in this work. Hope that this book would be successful.

**– GPH Panel of Experts**


## *Publisher's Note*

The lesson plan "Science" is prepared to apprise student on the formulation of the same. With the advent of technology and the Internet, there has been no dearth of information available to all; however, finding the relevant and qualitative information, which is focused, is an uphill task.

We at **GullyBaba Publishing House (P) Ltd.,** have taken this step to provide quality material which can accentuate in-depth knowledge about the subject. GPH books are a pioneer in the effort of providing unique and quality material to its readers. With our books, you are sure to attain success by making use of this powerful study material.

Our site **www.gullybaba.com** is a vital resource for your examination. The publisher wishes to acknowledge the significant contribution of the Team Members and our experts in bringing out this publication and highly thankful to Almighty God, without His blessings, this endeavor wouldn't have been successful.

**– Publisher**

# LESSON PLAN

# [SCIENCE]

## For B.Ed., JBT, DIET, PTT, NIT, BSTC, AND OTHERS

Gullybaba.com Amazon.in GPHbook.com

**Bestseller**

***Useful For***

IGNOU, Nalanda University, Kurushetra University, Lalit Narayan Mithila University, Andhra University, Pt. Sunderlal Sharma (Open) University (Bilaspur), Annamalai University, Bangalore University, Bharathiar University, Bharathidasan University, HP University, Jamia Millia Islamia, Kakatiya University (Andhra Pradesh), KSOU (Karnataka), KOU (Rajasthan), MPBOU (MP), MDU (Haryana), Punjab University, Tamilnadu Open University, Sri Padmavati Mahila Visvavidyalayam (Andhra Pradesh), Sri Venkateswara University (Andhra Pradesh), UCSDE (Kerala), University of Jammu, YCMOU, Rajasthan University, UPRTOU (UP) and all other Indian Universities.

**-Hindi Edition Also Available-**

GPH BOOK®

**GULLYBABA PUBLISHING HOUSE (P) LTD.**

ISO 9001:2008 & 14001:2004 CERTIFIED CO.

Published by:
**GullyBaba Publishing House Pvt. Ltd.**

**Regd. Office:**
2525/193, 1st Floor, Onkar Nagar-A,
Tri Nagar, Delhi-110035
(From Kanhaiya Nagar Metro Station Towards Old Bus Stand)
011-27387998, 27384836, 27385249
+919350849407

**Branch Office:**
1A/2A, 20, Hari Sadan,
Ansari Road, Daryaganj,
New Delhi-110002
Ph. 011-45794768

**E-mail:** hello@gullybaba.com, **Website**:GullyBaba.com

**New Edition**

**Price:** ₹200/-

**ISBN:** 978-93-82688-29-7
**Author:** GullyBaba.Com Panel

**Copyright© with Publisher**
All rights are reserved. No part of this publication may be reproduced or stored in a retrieval system or transmitted in any form or by any means; electronic, mechanical, photocopying, recording or otherwise, without the written permission of the copyright holder.
**Disclaimer:** Although the author and publisher have made every effort to ensure that the information in this book is correct, the author and publisher do not assume and hereby disclaim any liability to any party for any loss, damage, or disruption caused by errors or omissions, whether such errors or omissions result from negligence, accident, or any other cause.
If you find any kind of error, please let us know and get reward and or the new book free of cost.
The book is based on IGNOU syllabus. This is only a sample. The book/author/publisher does not impose any guarantee or claim for full marks or to be passed in exam. You are advised only to understand the contents with the help of this book and answer in your words.
All disputes with respect to this publication shall be subject to the jurisdiction of the Courts, Tribunals and Forums of New Delhi, India only.

**HOME DELIVERY of GPH Books**

You can get GPH books by VPP/COD/Speed Post/Courier.
You can order books by Email/SMS/WhatsApp/Call.
For more details, visit gullybaba.com/faq-books.html
Our packaging department usually dispatches the books within 2 days after receiving your order and it takes nearly 5-6 days in postal/courier services to reach your destination.

**Note:** Selling this book on any online platform like Amazon, Flipkart, Shopclues, Rediff, etc. without prior written permission of the publisher is prohibited and hence any sales by the SELLER will be termed as ILLEGAL SALE of GPH Books which will attract strict legal action against the offender.

# Topics Covered

# Contents

*"Teacher appreciation makes the world of education go around."*

*– Helen Peters*

# 1 Introduction

Planning is usually interpreted as a process to develop a strategy to achieve desired objectives, to solve problems and to facilitate action. It is equally true in relation to the teaching of any subject. Lesson plans will easily help one to achieve his/her goals and objectives and same can be said on the part of his/her students or pupils.

A lesson plan is a teacher's detailed description of the course of instruction for an individual lesson. A daily lesson plan is developed by a teacher to guide class instruction. The detail of the plan will vary depending on the preference of the teacher, subject being covered and the need and/or curiosity of children. There may be requirements mandated by the school system regarding the plan.

A well-developed lesson plan reflects the interests and needs of the students. It incorporates best practices for the educational field. The lesson plan correlates with the teacher's philosophy of education, which is what the teacher feels is the purpose of educating the students.

## Meaning of Lesson Planning

A lesson plan outlines in detail the various steps, which the teacher proposes to undertake in his/her class. As such, a lesson plan concerns itself with the teaching of one period. Planning for a lesson means identification of the sequence and style of presentation and evaluation procedure to be adopted for classroom teaching of a lesson. Hence, it is a proposition in advance which establishes a linkage between the why, what and how of teaching in one period. While attempting to do this, the teacher may foresee likely problems in classroom communication and may arrange certain materials and decide about techniques to be adopted to ensure a smooth and effective teaching-learning situation. Thus, a lesson plan is a means of taking advance decisions about the selection, sequencing and execution of various activities to be performed in a classroom with a view to ensuring learning of children.

## Need and Importance of Lesson Planning

When a teacher goes for teaching a lesson in the classroom, usually s/he gets prepared for it though informally. But sometimes, s/he finds that s/he is not able to teach the entire content which s/he prepared or on the other hand, the content to be covered is not sufficient for full period. Sometime, s/he may get stuck-up while teaching and so get nervous. May be that s/he is not aware of the objectives of teaching a lesson and so did not bother about its attainment. How to overcome all such problems? This can be done through systematic lesson planning. S/he gets a chance of thinking about all these problems in advance while planning his/her lesson and deciding about taking corrective steps for possible hurdles. The process of developing a lesson plan is such that these problems get tackled automatically.

Lesson planning helps the teacher in the following ways:

- It makes teaching systematic and well organised.
- It helps teachers in identifying adequate content and its proper sequencing for teaching a lesson.
- It helps teachers to learn to foresee and tackle learning difficulties of children.
- It enables teachers to utilise the available time properly.
- It helps in developing insights about learning needs and abilities of children.

- It helps teachers to develop the habit of undertaking immediate corrective measures.
- It gives confidence to teachers during teaching.

By lesson planning, following abilities can be improved in students:

- Questioning
- Defining a Problem
- Hypothesizing
- Planning a Solution
- Observing
- Discovering
- Discussing
- Recording
- Organising Knowledge
- Drawing Conclusions
- Generalising
- Understanding Relationship
- Using Previous Knowledge and Experience

## Steps of Lesson Planning

While developing a lesson plan, first of all a teacher has to decide about the objectives of teaching that particular lesson. The objectives will be both general as well as specific. In order to achieve the objectives, some subject matter or content is required. This content is to be selected as per the competence with reference to the specific objectives of the lesson as well as the previous knowledge of the learner. So the content has to be local specific, interesting and related to the previous knowledge of the learner. Another important aspect of lesson planning is to detail out the method to be used for transacting the required material to the learners. The choice of method will depend on the nature of the content, the class/grade as well as the ability of the learners. While specifying the method of delivery, the teachers' activities as well as the learners' activities are to be specified along with the evaluation exercises/questions. The evaluation has to be based on the material transacted in the classroom and the competency aimed to be developed. At the primary stage, the evaluation questions have to be very simple, keeping in view the learners' physical and mental growth.

The following issues need to be decided for developing a lesson plan:

- **Objectives:** The objectives of teaching a particular lesson should be stated as per the competency to be developed amongst children. Generally, teachers state only general and specific objectives of the lesson.
- **Content:** The subject matter that is intended to be covered should be limited to the prescribed time. The matter must be interesting and it should be related to the pupils' previous knowledge. It should also be related to daily life situations.
- **Methods:** The most appropriate method be chosen by the teacher. The selected method should be suitable to the subject matter to be taught. Suitable teaching aids must also be identified by the teacher. The teacher may also use supplementary aids to make his/her lesson more effective.
- **Evaluation:** A teacher must evaluate his/her lesson to find the extent to which he/she has achieved the objectives of his/her lesson. Evaluation can be done even by recapitulation of subject matter through suitable questions.

## Various Forms of Lesson Planning

These are various forms of written lesson plans in our country and abroad, but following three forms are most popular and most commonly used:

### (A) HERBARTIAN APPROACH TO LESSON PLANNING

The lesson planning is an ancient concept but still it has the important place in teacher education programmes in the teaching practices. In most of training institutions the Herbartian five steps approach of lesson planning is used.

"Johan Fredrik Herbart is a German philosopher and great Educational. He has divided teaching unit activities into five steps. His approach is theoretically based on appreciative mass theory of learning. Therefore, he gives more emphasis of teacher presentation." It appears from its structure that Classical Human OrganisationTheory influences this approach. The previous knowledge of student is considered in preparing a lesson plan but their abilities, interests, attitudes and values are not taken into consideration in designing a lesson plan. The teacher is organised at memory–level. This approach has the wider use in the teaching of various school subjects.

Under this approach the following five steps are employed:

- Preparation
- Presentation
- Comparison and abstraction
- Generalisation and
- Application.

**Outline of Lesson Plan**

An outline of a lesson plan has been developed on the basis of these five steps in the following forms:

- Subject, topic, class with section, period and date.
- General objectives of the teaching subject,
- Specific objectives related to the topic,
- Introduction,
- Statement of aim,
- Presentation including developing questions,
- Explanation,
- Black Board Summary,
- Review, questions or Recapulatory questions, and
- Homework or assignment.

The above teaching points are followed to prepare a lesson to teach:

**(1) Subjects, Topic and Class**

A teacher selects a topic for the teaching of his own interest. He decides the data period and section of his class. These details are written in preparing his lesson–plan. This step also delimits his lesson plan.

**(2) General Objectives of the Teaching Subject**

The different school subjects have their own general objectives. The topic is taught at different levels but these levels have different objectives. The teacher has to write the general objective of his subjects considering the level of the students. These general objectives can be achieved by organising teaching for a period of forty minutes duration.

**(3) Specific Objectives**

A Lesson plan is prepared for achieving learning objectives, which are concerned with general objectives of teaching. The specific objectives may be knowledge skills and appreciations. The social studies lesson is designed for achieving knowledge objectives, poetry lesson for appreciation and language, craft and home science for skill. These are written in behavioural terms.

**(4) Introduction**

This step mainly concern with starting points of teaching activities. The teacher employs his insight and experiences for linking new knowledge with the previous knowledge of the students. Preparing introductory questions may use the priming and prompting devices. The topic is usually emitted by the student's responses by asking questions or creating appropriate situation.

**(5) Statement of Aim**

An introductory stage, the efforts are made for emitting the topic from the students. The teacher gives his statement of teaching topic by incorporating the student responses.

**(6) Presentation**

The teacher prepares developing questions after introducing the topic to be taught. The presentation is done with the help of developing questions. The questions are arranged in a logical sequence keeping in view the structure of teaching unit.

**(7) Explanation**

When the students are not able to answer the developing questions of teacher, he is supposed to explain the element or concept by giving the statements.

**(8) Blackboard Summary**

The teacher has to prepare the blackboard summary of his teaching points and explanations.

**(9) Recapulatory Questions**

The students should note down the Blackboard summary. The black board summary must be removed before asking the recapulatory questions. The purpose of these questions is to practice the student learning and evaluate the student's performance to know that they could comprehend the teaching unit.

**(10) Homework**

At the end of lesson plan, some homework is assigned to the students on the same topic. The purpose of homework is to practice, to organise and to study the topic. The students get an opportunity for assimilation with the help of homework or assignments.

**Advantages of Herbartian Lesson Planning**

The following are major advantages of Herbartian five steps of lesson planning:

- It is logical and psychological. It incorporates the principles of learning.
- It is employed in the teaching for all school subject social studies, languages, English and Science subjects.
- It employs the deductive and inductive method of teaching.
- It is useful for achieving the cognitive objectives of teaching.
- It is simple and easy approach of lesson planning.
- It employs the previous knowledge of the students for imparting new knowledge.

**Demerits of Herbartian Lesson Planning**

The Herbartian lesson planning is most popular but it has the following demerits:

- It is highly dominated by the teacher.
- It is highly structured and does not provide the opportunities for learner's creativity and originality.
- It is highly located by cognitive objectives but cannot be effectively employed for affective and psychomotor objectives.
- It does not consider the learning-structures in organising teaching activities.
- The specific objectives are not written in behavioural terms.
- The teaching activities are less meaningful and practical.

## (B) BLOOM'S OR EVALUATION APPROACH TO LESSON PLANNING

The evaluation approach is a new innovation in the field of education. It has revolutionised the teaching, learning and testing process. It considers that education is the tricolour process.

This approach has the following features:

- The education is a purposeful process. All the educational Activities are objective-centred.
- The testing should be based on teaching. The teaching and testing should be objective oriented.
- The term evaluation concerns with all activities of teaching and testing and not only students performances.
- It does not confine to the students achievement only but it includes the total behaviour change of the students.
- It evaluates the teaching-learning objectives, methods and devices of providing learning experiences.

- The student's performances are measured in terms of learning objectives and not the achievement of the content. It may cover cognitive, affective and psychomotor learning outcomes used.

B.S. Bloom has given this approach to teaching learning. The following three steps are:

- Formulating Educational Objectives,
- Creation Learning Experiences, and
- Evaluating the Change of behaviours.

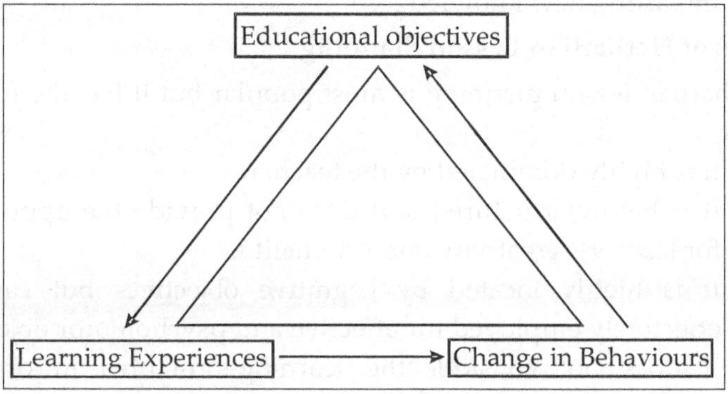


**Fig. 1.1: Tripolar Process**

**Formulating Formulation of Educational Objectives**

The end result of any activity is known as objective. The well-organised activity brings a desirable change, which is termed as objective. The educational objectives concern with collative, affective and psychomotor change in the behaviours. The following things should be kept in mind in identifying and formulating educational objectives:

- The nature of various school subjects in significantly different. Thus, different-objectives are achieved by teaching the various school subjects.
- The structure of the content, students level and need, social and economic conditions, practical and cultural needs are the basis for determining the objectives of teaching.
- The student's growth and development should be kept in view in formulating the objectives of learning, because the same contents are taught at different stage of development.
- The student entering behaviours and their comprehension levels are considered in formulating learning objectives.

- The objectives are written in behavioural terms after identifying them. The procedure is followed in formulating and writing objectives in behavioural form.

**Creating Learning Experiences**

After identifying the learning objective, the appropriate teaching strategies, teaching aids and tactics are selected for generating the environments for providing the learning experiences to the students. The learning experiences are directly related to the objectives of teaching. These learning experiences may be provided in the school or classroom and outside the school. A teacher organises his/her activities for bringing the desirable change among the students. The teaching activities are related to learning outcomes. This concept has been illustrated with the help of the following way:

The table indicates that employing different type of teaching strategies for achieving different learning objectives provides different types of learning experiences.

**Table 1.1**

| S.No. | Teaching Objectives | Learning Experiences |
|---|---|---|
| (1) | Knowledge Objective | Lecturing Telling, showing, demonstration, Chart, models, text book, programmed instruction, homework, and assignments |
| (2) | Understanding Objective | Question-answer strategy, group discussion, Line drawing, Map, Models, Text Books, Homework and assignments. |
| (3) | Application Objective | Project Method, Tutorials, Inter action strategy, Text Book, Homework, and assignments. |
| (4) | Creativity Objective | Problem solving, method individual experimentation, Seminar and workshop, etc. |

**Evaluating change of Behaviours**

The learning experiences bring desirable change in behaviour of the students. The change of behaviours is evaluated to take decision about the effectiveness of learning experiences. The change of behaviours is of three types: cognitive, affective and psychomotor. A criterion test is prepared for measuring all the three types of objectives. The objective and essay type tests are constructed for measuring cognitive objectives. The oral questions are used in lesson planning. The following measuring devices are used. For evaluating cognitive, psychomotor and affective objectives:

**Table 1.2**

| S.No. | Learning Objectives | Evaluation Devices |
|---|---|---|
| (1) | Cognitive | Oral, observation, written essay and objective type tests and interview. |
| (2) | Affective | Observation, interest inventory, attitude scale, value test, essay type test and situational test. |
| (3) | Psychomotor | Observation, practical examination, student demonstration and interview. |

It is evident from the table that different types of measuring instruments and devices are employed for evaluating three types of objectives. The change of behaviour is the empirical criterion for the effective use of teaching strategies, tactics and teaching aids which have been used for providing the learning experiences.

**Merits of Bloom's Lesson Planning**

The following are the main characteristics of lesson planning:

- The content analysis is done and two-dimensional charts are prepared for specifying the objectives.
- The objectives are written in behavioural terms.
- The teaching activities are organised for achieving these objectives.
- The teaching activities are related to the learning structures.
- This type of Lesson plan makes the teaching purposeful and objective centred.
- It is based on psychological and scientific principles.
- It has the greater scope for improving and modifying the learning experience on teaching activities.

**Demerits of Bloom's Lesson Planning**

This has the following demerits:

- This approach of lesson planning is highly structured and mechanised and does not provide an opportunity for creativity and originality of the teacher.
- It has the greater scope for personal factors of teacher influence the planning and organising teaching activities.
- One teaching activity does not confine to one domain. It concerns with more than one domain.
- The mental process or mental abilities are not taken into consideration in writing objectives in behavioural term.

## (C) RCEM APPROACH TO LESSON PLANNING

The Indian educationists develop this approach of lesson planning. This is an improvement over the earlier approaches. It also considers the Bloom's Taxonomy of Educational objectives in identifying objective of teaching with certain modification. RCEM approach involves seventeen mental abilities for writing objectives in functional form.

The structure of lesson plan is developed with help of input, process and output aspects of teaching.

**Input**

It includes the identification of objectives. They are known as Expected Behavioural Outcomes (EBOs). These objectives are broadly classified into four categories: knowledge, understanding, application and creativity. These objectives are written in behavioural terms by employing seventeen mental abilities. The entering behaviours of the learners are also identified. The sequence of instructional procedure is determined with the help of these objectives.

**Process**

The teaching strategies and tactics are selected for achieving these objectives. The communication strategy and audio-visual aids are employed for the effective presentation of the content. The main focus of the process is to create the learning situations for providing appropriate learning experiences to the students. The process also includes the technique of motivation so that student's behaviour can be reinforced for the desirable responses. It implies the interaction of teacher and students. The participation of pupils and teacher is essential.

**Output**

This aspect of instructional procedure includes the Real Learning outcomes (RLOs). Learning experiences are provided for the desirable Behavioural change among students, the change of the behaviours is known as real learning outcomes. The various measuring devices are employed for evaluating RLOs. The measuring instruments are constructed on the basis of EBOs. The teacher usually measures the RLOs by using oral and writing questions.

**Merits of RCEM Approach**

- More suitable to our schools, as it has been developed in our country.

- Use of mental processes in place of action worlds while writing the instructional objectives.
- The focus on the process, not on product while writing objectives.
- Evaluation task in quite simple and objective.

**Demerits of RCEM Approach**

- Time consuming approach.
- Suitable to cognitive objectives only, no dealing with affective and psychomotor objectives.
- The whole learning of human being cannot be explained fully through only 17 mental abilities.
- This approach is an improvement over the prevailing practices of lesson planning.

## Limitations of Lesson Planning

- It makes teaching organised but rigid.
- If followed strictly, it leaves no room for innovativeness on the part of the teacher.
- Too much of emphasis on it may make things routinised.
- It is good for beginner teachers. Experienced teachers usually have little faith in structured classroom behaviours.
- It is difficult to anticipate all possible kinds of classroom situations in advance and therefore lesson plans lack relevance.

✍✍✍

*"In learning you will teach, and in teaching you will learn."*

*– Phil Collins*

# 2 Teaching of Science

"It took me hours to plan my first lesson. I was suddenly aware of all things you have to deal with when teaching science. You need to think about things like giving out lab books, children not having pens and pencils and getting out and packing away equipment as well as researching and presenting your subject in a clear and uncluttered way. When I started teaching, my lesson plans were extremely detailed. I planned for every little classroom event; however, as my practice progressed I was able to focus my planning on key aspects of the lesson. Things like taking the register, giving out books and packing away equipment become automatic after a while."

**– (Peter, a trainee biology teacher, recorded during a PGCE science course)**

## What is Science?

Science can be defined in the following manner:

- Science is a systematised knowledge of our environment.
- Science is man's systematic investigation of his environment.
- Albert Einstein opines, "The whole of science is nothing more than a refinement of everyday thinking".
- Science involves describing, predicting and explaining nature and its changes in the simplest way possible.

# Nature of Teaching and Learning Science

The nature of teaching and learning science includes the following aspects:

**(1) The concept of open competence:** In the development of a school science programme, especially for teacher educators, the concept of open competence may include the process skills or scientific methods, which has the following components.

(a) Observation

(b) Formulation of hypothesis

(c) Designing of experiments

(d) Measurement, recording

(e) Inference

(f) Generalisation

(g) Formulating models

**(2) Comprehension of fundamentals of science (as against memorisation):** More emphasis should be given to the comprehension of the fundamentals of science as against memorisation. This implies that the basic aim of science teaching, especially at the social level, is to supply basic knowledge of science, which may be brought into use in the daily environment through study and application of science. This may also provide a systematic, practical and balanced view of the discipline of science to change students' behaviour through their knowledge. A holistic view of science is imperative to present "Balanced Science for All" which may include the following:

(a) Concepts in science,

(b) Processes of science,

(c) Social and cultural aspects of science, and

(d) Moral and ethical aspects of science.

**(3) Science as a way of thinking:** Teaching of science at the school level may encourage permeation of the spirit of science as a way of thinking. To accomplish this, one may take the help of the following approaches to scientific thinking.

(a) Discovery/Inquiry/Investigation

(b) Divergent and convergent

(c) Analytical and synthetic

(d) Imaginative and creative

**(4) Development of scientific attitudes, temper and habits:** The science teachers all over the world have long recognised that proper scientific attitudes are among the important outcomes, which are the result of science teaching. They are becoming aware that if scientific attitudes are to be developed from the study of science, they must be taught directly and systematically in the same manner as we try to develop a mastery of the principles of science itself.

The development of scientific attitudes could be demonstrated as the ability to do the following:

(a) To view facts objectively

(b) To be free from dogma and superstitions

(c) To revise one's opinion as evidence warrants

(d) To have a spirit of inquiry

(e) To be open-minded

The amount of success in developing scientific attitudes are depends ultimately upon the teachers and it is important that the science teacher should always keep in mind that students form attitudes more from the examples taken from everyday life than from abstract percepts. In the 'Third World' countries especially, rural people have certain superstitions about diet, astrology, medicine and the like. These superstitions and beliefs should be dealt properly with the help of students when they reveal the truth to the masses.

A vitalised study of science with its emphasis on open-mindedness, tolerance and objectivity will inevitably lead to the development of a more secular outlook in true sense. This can instill the sense of responsibility among those who profess different religions.

The above-mentioned discussion suggests the need to develop attitudes, such as self-confidence and self-reliance and to have a holistic view of science, a view of the social, cultural, moral and ethical aspects of science.

**(3) Science and values:** As mentioned earlier, there is a great danger in science if it is treated as a singular value system.

Therefore, we have to recognise science as an important tool to solve our social problems and also as an important component of the cultural, social and spiritual heritage. The correlation between science and values is immense and needs to be properly addressed.

## Aims of Teaching and Learning Science

Science teaches us an understanding of natural phenomena. It aims to stimulate a child's curiosity in finding out why things happen in the way that they do. It teaches methods of inquiry and investigation to stimulate creative thoughts. Children learn to ask scientific questions and begin to appreciate the way in which science will affect the future on a personal, national and global level. Thus, we can say that without science, general education is incomplete. The main objective of teachers is to teach science effectively, so that the students are able to impart the liberal education. It helps teacher to acquaint pupils with the broad outline of great scientific principles and ways to exemplified science in the service of man, to earn the living, to become cleverer and more intelligent. In the science teaching, the teacher's attitudes towards the marvels of sciences are important in as much as pupils copy their teachers in attitude development. While these facts of science are important, it is also important that pupils should understand the system of observation, guess and experiment, which is known as scientific method. So, one of the aims of science teaching is to explain this method and to help pupils to think correctly about science in relation to other subjects of learning. These aims of science education in schools mentioned above can be achieved by the combined teaching in the classroom and the laboratory.

*"Those who know, do. These that understand, teach."*

*– Aristotle*

# 3 Different Lesson Planning

## LESSON PLAN – 1

| | |
|---|---|
| **Subject:** Science | **Date:** ______ |
| **Topic:** Photosynthesis | **Duration:** 35 – 40 minutes |
| | **Class:** 7th |

**(1) General Objectives**

- To develop the interest of students in learning science.
- To develop the abilities of imagination, reasoning and observation.
- To inculcate creativity in students.
- To develop the understanding about the reality and observation.
- To enable them to get knowledge contained in the lesson.

**(2) Specific Objectives**

- To make students aware about how water and minerals absorbed by roots reach the leaves.
- To enable the students to describe the process of photosynthesis.

- To enable the students to draw a schematic diagram showing photosynthesis.
- To enable the students to know the specialty about the leaves that they can synthesise food but other parts of the plant cannot.
- To enable the students to observe some plants with deep red, violet or brown leaves and show that these leaves also carry out photosynthesis by an activity.

**(3) Previous Knowledge**

The students must have at least general familiarities with nutrients; mode of nutrition in plants, i.e. autotrophic nutrition, heterotrophic nutrition, etc.

**(4) Teaching Aids**

Blackboard, chalk, duster, pointer, models of photosynthesis process, chemicals and equipments, etc.

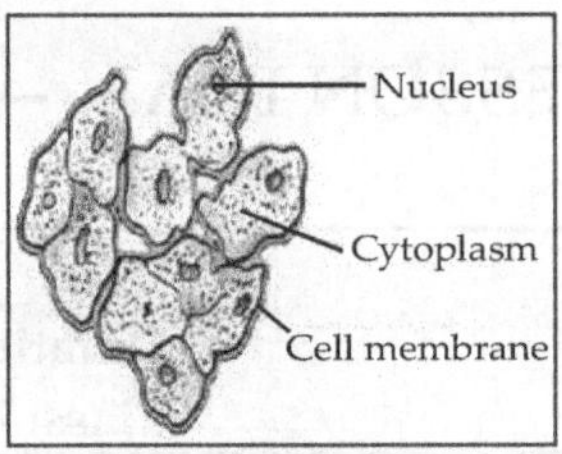


**Fig. 3.1: Cell**

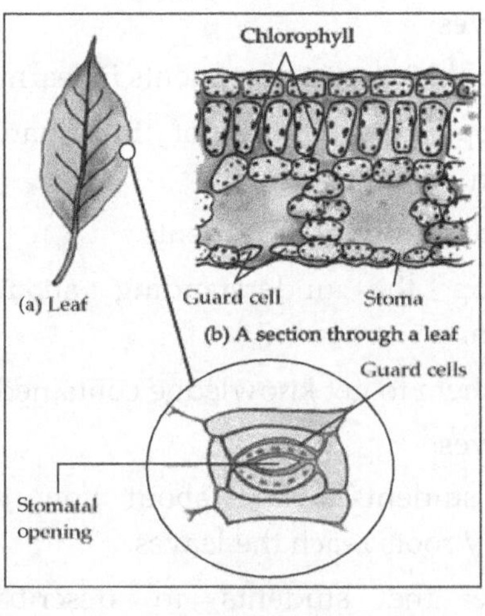


**Fig. 3.2: Stomata**

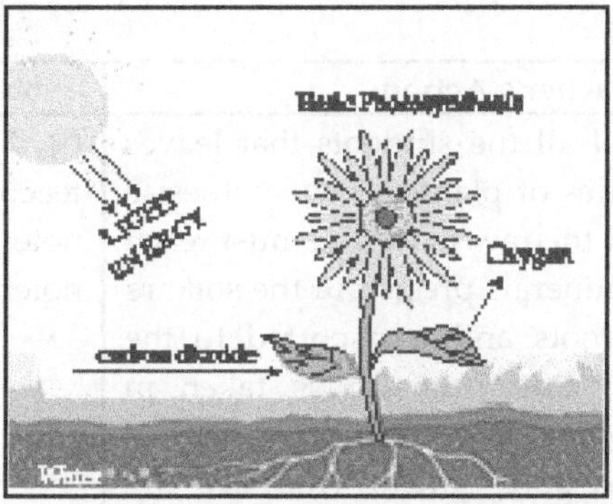


**Fig. 3.3: Schematic diagram showing photosynthesis**

## (5) Introduction

| Teacher's Question | Student's Answer |
|---|---|
| (i) What is nutrient? | (i) It is a substance that provides essential nourishment for growth and the maintenance of life. |
| (ii) Tell the modes of nutrients in plants. | (ii) Two modes of nutrients in plants, i.e. autotrophic and heterotrophic nutrition. |
| (iii) What do you know about autotrophic nutrition? | (iii) Nutrition in which organisms make their own food from simple substances is called autotrophic nutrition. |
| (iv) What do you know about heterotrophic nutrition? | (iv) Nutrition in which organisms take in readymade food prepared by the plants are called heterotrophs. |
| (v) Where the food factories of plants are located? | (v) ………………… |
| (vi) Whether food is made in all parts of a plant or only in a certain part? | (vi) ………………… |
| (vii) How do plants obtain the raw materials from the surroundings? | (vii) ………………… |
| (viii) How do they transport them to the food factories of the plants? | (viii) ………………… |

## (6) Statement of topic

Now, teacher will announce the topic, "Today, we will study about photosynthesis process."

**(7) Presentation**

| Teacher's Action | Student's Activity |
|---|---|
| (i) Teacher will tell all the students that leaves are the food factories of plants. They synthesise food. Therefore, all the raw materials must reach there. Water and minerals present in the soil are absorbed by the roots and transported to the leaves. Carbon dioxide from air is taken in through the tiny pores present on the surface of the leaves. These pores are surrounded by 'guard cells'. Such pores are called stomata. | (i) After listening the teacher, students will note it down in their notebooks. |
| (ii) Teacher will tell that now I teach you about cells. You have seen that buildings are made of bricks. Similarly, the bodies of living organisms are made of tiny units called cells. Cells can be seen only under the microscope. Some organisms are made of only one cell. The cell is enclosed by a thin outer boundary, called the cell membrane. Most cells have a distinct, centrally located spherical structure called the nucleus. The nucleus is surrounded by a jelly-like substance called cytoplasm. | (ii) Students will note it down in their notebooks. Some students ask that how water and minerals absorbed by roots reach the leaves. |
| (iii) Teacher will tell that water and minerals are transported to the leaves by the vessels, which run like pipes throughout the root, the stem, the branches and the leaves. They form a continuous path or passage for the nutrients to reach the leaf. | (iii) Students will note it down in their notebooks. Some students ask that what is so special about the leaves that they synthesise food but other parts of the plant do not. |
| (iv) Teacher will tell that the leaves have a green pigment called chlorophyll. It helps leaves to capture the energy of the sunlight. This energy is used to synthesise (prepare) food from carbon dioxide and water. Since the synthesis of food occurs in the presence of sunlight, it is called **photosynthesis** (Photo: light; synthesis: to combine). So, we find that chlorophyll, sunlight, carbon dioxide and water are necessary to carry out the process of photosynthesis. It is a unique | (iv) Students will note it down in their notebooks. |

| | |
|---|---|
| process on the earth. The solar energy is captured by the leaves and stored in the plant in the form of food. Thus, Sun is the ultimate source of energy for all living organisms. | |
| (v) Teacher will tell that during photosynthesis, chlorophyll containing cells of leaves, in the presence of sunlight, use carbon dioxide and water to synthesise carbohydrates. This process can be represented as an equation: Carbon dioxide + water $\xrightarrow[\text{chlorophyll}]{\text{sunlight}}$ carbohydrate + oxygen During the process, oxygen is released. The carbohydrates ultimately get converted into starch. The presence of starch in leaves indicates the occurrence of photosynthesis. The starch is also a carbohydrate. | (v) Students will note it down in their note-books. |

**(8) Experiment**

| Activity | Discussion | Result |
|---|---|---|
| Take two potted plants of the same kind. Keep one in the dark (or in a black box) for 72 hours and the other in the sunlight. Perform iodine test with the leaves of both the plants. | Record your results. | After performing iodine test, the plant kept in sunlight de-colourises. |
| Now leave the pot, which was earlier kept in the dark, in the sunlight for 3 – 4 days and perform the iodine test again on its leaves. | Record your observations in your note-book. | We will find that the plant in sunlight have blue colour-ation in the green patches of the leaves indicating the presence of starch by photo-synthesis in the green areas only. This shows the pre-sence of chlorophyll in the leaves of the plant, which indicates that photosyn-thesis, occurs in these plants. |

**(9) Recapitulation**

- Why do organisms need to take food?
- How would you test the presence of starch in leaves?
- Give a brief description of the process of synthesis of food in green plants.

**(10) Homework**

(1) Show with the help of a sketch that the plants are the ultimate source of food.

(2) Fill in the blanks:

(a) Green plants are called _______ since they synthesise their own food.

(b) The food synthesised by the plants is stored as _______.

(c) In photosynthesis, solar energy is captured by the pigment called _______.

(d) During photosynthesis, plants take in _______ and release _______.

> **TO THIS END THE GREATEST ASSET OF A SCHOOL IS THE PERSONALITY OF THE TEACHER.**
>
> — **Maggie Gallagher**

# LESSON PLAN – 2

| | |
|---|---|
| **Subject:** Science | **Date:** ________ |
| **Topic:** Clinical Thermometer | **Duration:** 35 – 40 minutes |
| | **Class:** 7th |

**(1) General Objectives**

- To develop the interest of students in learning science.
- To develop the abilities of imagination, reasoning and observation.
- To inculcate creativity in students.
- To develop the understanding about the reality and observation.
- To enable them to get knowledge contained in the lesson.

**(2) Specific Objectives**

- To enable the students to read the temperature from a thermometer.
- To enable the students to draw the diagram of a thermometer.
- To enable the students to describe the construction and working of the thermometer.
- To enable the students to describe what precautions should be taken while reading a clinical thermometer.
- To enable the students to learn about the normal temperature of human body.

**(3) Previous Knowledge**

The students must have at least a general familiarity with the concepts like hot and cold objects, temperature, etc.

**(4) Teaching Aids**

Blackboard, chalk, duster, pointer, clinical thermometer, etc.

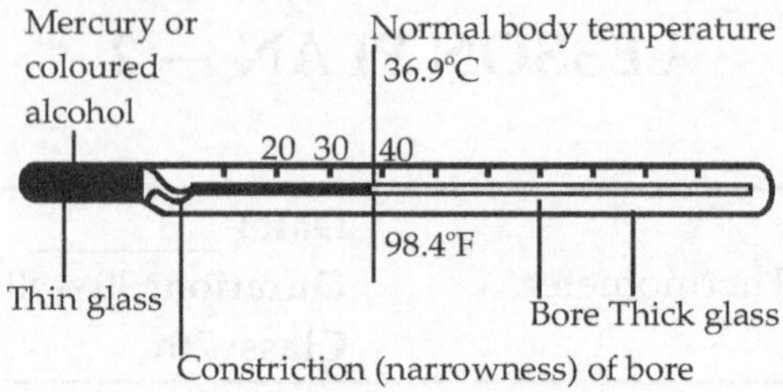


**Fig. 3.4: A clinical thermometer**

**Table 3.1: Hot and cold objects**

| Object | Cold/Cool | Warm/Hot |
|---|---|---|
| Ice cream | √ | |
| Spoon in a tea cup | | |
| Fruit juice | | |
| Handle of a frying pan | | |

**Table 3.2:**

| Name | Temperature (°C) |
|---|---|
| Prachi | 37°C |
| Nadeem | 37.5°C |
| Jainab | 37.1°C |
| Kirti | 37.05°C |
| Shankar | 36.80°C |
| Shakti | 36.90°C |
| Sonia | 37.01°C |
| Sita | 37.02°C |
| Tripti | 37.2°C |
| Mehul | 37°C |

**(5) Introduction**

| Teacher's Question | Student's Answer |
|---|---|
| (i) How do we know whether an object is hot or cold? | (i) By touching them. |
| (ii) Mark the objects as hot or cold, given in the table 3.1. | (ii) Ice cream is a cool object. |

| | |
|---|---|
| (iii) What do you know about temperature? | (iii) It expresses the common notions of hot and cold. |
| (iv) How do we find out how hot an object really is? | (iv) By its temperature. |
| (v) Which device is used to measure a temperature? | (v) Thermometer. |
| (vi) What do you know about clinical thermometer? | (vi) ............................ |

**(6) Statement of topic**

Now, teacher will announce the topic, "Today, we will study about clinical thermometer."

**(7) Presentation**

| Teacher's Action | Student's Activity |
|---|---|
| (i) Teacher will tell all the students that the thermometer, which measures our body temperature, is called a clinical thermometer. | (i) After listening teacher, students will note it down in their note-books. |
| (ii) Teacher will tell that a clinical thermometer looks like the one shown in Fig. 3.4. | (ii) Students will draw its rough diagram into their notebooks. |
| (iii) Teacher will tell that a clinical thermometer consists of a long, narrow, uniform glass tube. It has a bulb at one end. This bulb contains mercury. Outside the bulb, a small shining thread of mercury can be seen. | (iii) Students will note it down in their notebooks. |
| (iv) If you do not see the mercury thread, rotate the thermometer a bit till you see it. You will also find a scale on the thermometer. The scale we use is the Celsius scale, indicated by °C. A clinical thermometer reads temperature from 35°C to 42°C. | (iv) Students will note it down in their notebooks. |
| (v) Teacher will tell some pre-cautions that should be taken while reading a clinical thermometer: | (v) Students will note it down in their notebooks. |

| | |
|---|---|
| • Thermometer should be washed before and after use, preferably with an anti-septic solution.<br>• Ensure that before use the mercury level is below 35°C.<br>• Read the thermometer keeping the level of mercury along the line of sight.<br>• Handle the thermometer with care. If it hits against some hard object, it can break.<br>• Don't hold the thermometer by the bulb while reading it. | |

**(8) Experiment**

| Activity | Discussion | Result |
|---|---|---|
| Measure the body temperature of some of your friends (at least 10) with a clinical thermometer. Record your observations as in Table 3.2. | Is the body temperature of every person 37°C? | The temperature of every person may not be 37°C. It could be slightly higher or slightly lower. Actually, what we call normal temperature is the average body temperature of a large number of healthy persons. |

**(9) Recapitulation**

- How would you measure the temperature of a body?
- What precautions should be taken while using a thermometer?

**(10) Homework**

Fill in the blanks:

- The hotness of an object is determined by its __________.
- Temperature is measured in degree ____________.
- Normal temperature of the human body is ___________.

# LESSON PLAN – 3

| | |
|---|---|
| **Subject:** Science | **Date:** ________ |
| **Topic:** Rusting of iron and crystallisation | **Duration:** 35 – 40 minutes |
| | **Class:** 7th |

**(1) General Objectives**

- To develop the interest of students in learning science.
- To develop the abilities of imagination, reasoning and observation.
- To inculcate creativity in students.
- To develop the understanding about the reality and observation.
- To enable them to get knowledge contained in the lesson.

**(2) Specific Objectives**

- To enable the students to learn across many changes in surroundings.
- To enable the students to demonstrate the nature of these changes.
- To enable the students to perform some activities related to changes.
- To enable the students to observe rusting of iron.
- To enable the students to observe the process of crystallisation.

**(3) Previous Knowledge**

The students must have at least general familiarities with changes, its kinds and nature.

**(4) Teaching Aids**

Blackboard, chalk, duster, pointer, water, dilute sulphuric acid, copper sulphate and equipments related to activities, etc.

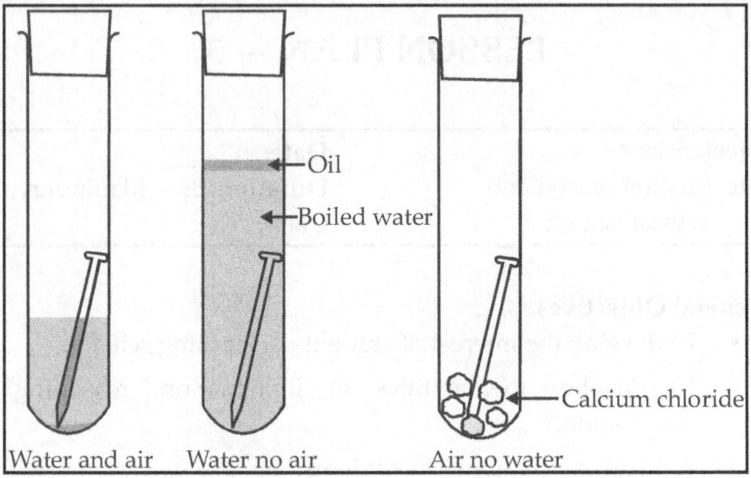


**Fig. 3.5: Rusting of Iron**

**Fig. 3.6: Crystals of copper sulphate**

### (5) Introduction

| Teacher's Question | Student's Answer |
|---|---|
| (i) What do you know about changes? | (i) Every day we come across many changes in our surroundings. These changes may involve one or more substances. For example, making a sugar solution is a change. |
| (ii) How many types of changes are there? | (ii) Two, i.e. physical and chemical. |
| (iii) What is a physical change? | (iii) When a new substance is formed. |
| (iv) Give some examples of physical change. | (iv) Crumpling a sheet or paper, breaking a pane of glass, freezing water into ice, etc. |

| | |
|---|---|
| (v) What is a chemical change? | (v) When one or more new substances are formed. It is also known as a chemical reaction. |
| (vi) Give some examples of chemical changes. | (vi) Burning a log of wood, mixing an acid with a base, producing water and a salt and photosynthesis (a process in which carbon dioxide and water are changed into sugars by plants.) |
| (vii) What do you know about rusting of iron? | (vii) .............................. |
| (viii) What do you know about crystallisation? | (viii) .............................. |

**(6) Statement of topic**

Now, teacher will announce the topic, "Today, we will study about rusting of iron and crystallisation."

**(7) Presentation**

| Teacher's Action | Student's Activity |
|---|---|
| (i) Teacher will tell all the students that if you leave a piece of iron in the open for some time, it acquires a film of brownish substance. This substance is called rust and the process is called rusting. Iron gates of parks or farmlands, iron benches kept in lawns and gardens, almost every article of iron, kept in the open gets rusted. At home, you must have seen shovels and spades getting rusted when exposed to the atmosphere for some time. In the kitchen, a wet iron pan (tawa) often gets rusted if left in that state for some time. Rust is not iron. It is different from iron on which it gets deposited. | (i) After listening the teacher, students will note it down in their notebooks. |
| (ii) Teacher will tell that rusting of iron is one change that affects iron articles and slowly destroys them. | (ii) Students will note it down in their notebooks. |
| (iii) Teacher will tell that the process of rusting can be represented by the following equation: | (iii) Students will note down the equation in their note-books. |

| | |
|---|---|
| $\text{Iron(Fe)} + \text{Oxygen}(O_2, \text{from the air}) + \text{Water}(H_2O) \rightarrow \text{Rust(Iron oxide } Fe_2O_3)$ | |
| (iv) Teacher will tell that the presence of both oxygen and water (or water vapour) is essential for rusting. In fact, if the content of moisture in air is high, which means if it is more humid, rusting becomes faster. | (iv) Students will note it down in their notebooks. Some students may ask that how do we prevent rusting; prevent iron articles from coming in contact with oxygen or water or both. |
| (v) Teacher will tell that one simple way is to apply a coat of paint or grease. In fact, these coats should be applied regularly to | (v) Students will note it down in their notebooks. |
| (vi) Teacher will tell that, as you know that salt can be obtained by the evaporation of seawater. The salt obtained in this manner is not pure and its crystals are small. The shape of the crystals cannot be seen clearly. However, large crystals of pure substances can be formed from their solutions. The process is called crystallisation. It is an example of a physical change. | (vi) Students will note it down in their notebooks. |

**(8) Experiment**

| Activity | Discussion | Result |
|---|---|---|
| Take a cupful of water in a beaker and add a few drops of dilute sulphuric acid. Heat the water. When it starts boiling, add copper sulphate powder slowly while stirring continuously. Continue adding copper sulphate powder until no more powder can be dissolved. Filter the solution. Allow it to cool. Do not disturb | Look at the solution after some time. Can you see the crystals of copper sulphate? If not, wait for some more time. | After cooling, the crystals of copper sulphate are seen. Due to its change in its physical properties, this type of change is a physical change. |

| the solution when it is cooling. | | |
|---|---|---|

**(9) Recapitulation**

- Classify the changes involved in the following processes as physical or chemical changes:
  - Photosynthesis
  - Dissolving sugar in water
  - Burning of coal
  - Melting of wax
  - Beating aluminium to make aluminium foil
  - Digestion of food
- State whether the following statements are true or false. In case a statement is false, write the correct statement in your notebook.
  - Cutting a log of wood into pieces is a chemical change. (True/False)
  - Formation of manure from leaves is a physical change. (True/False)

**(10) Homework**

- When a candle burns, both physical and chemical changes take place. Identify these changes. Give another example of a familiar process in which both the chemical and physical changes take place.
- Describe how crystals of copper sulphate are prepared.
- Explain how painting of an iron gate prevents it from rusting.
- Explain why rusting of iron objects is faster in coastal areas than in deserts.

# LESSON PLAN – 4

| **Subject:** Science | **Date:** ________ |
|---|---|
| **Topic:** Types and Properties of Soil | **Duration:** 35 – 40 minutes |
| | **Class:** 7th |

### (1) General Objectives

- To develop the interest of students in learning science.
- To develop the abilities of imagination, reasoning and observation.
- To inculcate creativity in students.
- To develop the understanding about the reality and observation.
- To enable them to get knowledge contained in the lesson.

### (2) Specific Objectives

- To enable the students to know about the different types of soil.
- To enable the students to find the characteristics of soil.
- To enable the students to find different uses of soil.
- To enable the students to know about percolation rate of water in soil.
- To enable the students to give formula of rate of percolation.

### (3) Previous Knowledge

The students must have at least general familiarities with soil, soil profile and layers of soil.

### (4) Teaching Aids

Blackboard, chalk, duster, pointer, samples of clayey, loamy and sandy soils, hollow cylinder or a pipe and other useful equipments, etc.

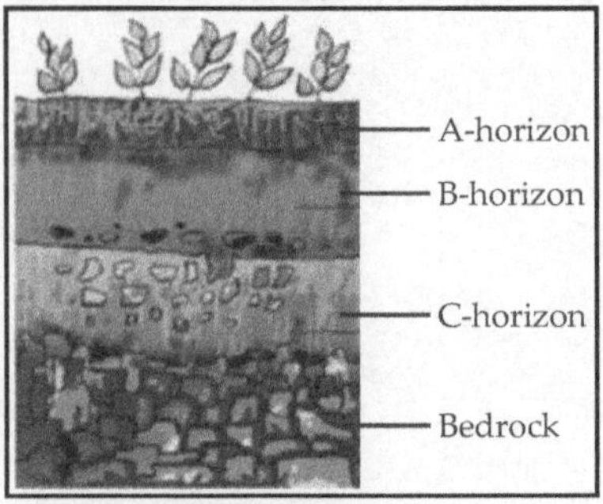


**Fig. 3.7: Soil Profile**

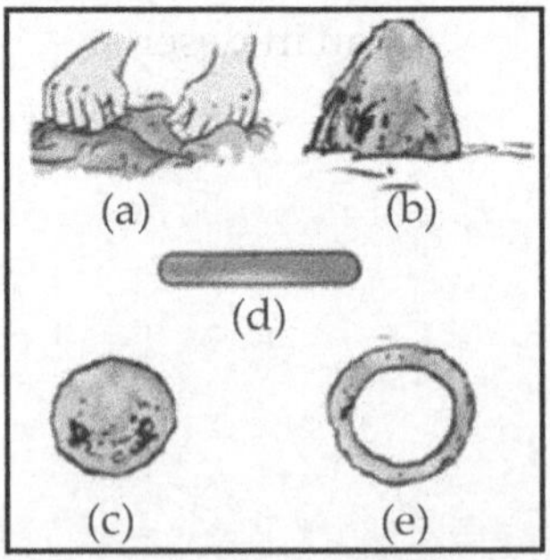


**Fig. 3.8: Working with the soil**

**Fig. 3.9: Measuring rate of percolation**

**(5) Introduction**

| Teacher's Question | Student's Answer |
|---|---|
| (i) What do you know about soil? | (i) The mixture of rock particles and humus is called the soil. |
| (ii) What are the different layers of soil? | (ii) Soil is made up of distinct layers, called horizons. The different layers of soil are O Horizon, A Horizon, B Horizon and C Horizon. |
| (iii) What do you know about soil profile? | (iii) A vertical section through different layers of the soil is called the soil profile. |
| (iv) Can you classify the soil on the basis of the proportion of particles of various sizes. | (iv) ..................... |
| (v) Give some characteristics of soil. | (v) ..................... |

**(6) Statement of topic**

Now, teacher will announce the topic, "Today, we will study about types and properties of soil."

**(7) Presentation**

| Teacher's Action | Student's Activity |
|---|---|
| (i) Teacher will tell all the students that the soil is classified based on the proportion of particles of various sizes. | (i) After listening teacher, students will note it down in their notebooks. |
| (ii) Teacher will tell that if soil contains greater proportion of big particles it is called sandy soil. If the proportion of fine particles is relatively higher, then it is called clayey soil. If the amount of large and fine particles is about the same, then the soil is | (ii) Students will note it down in their notebooks. |

| | |
|---|---|
| called loamy. Thus, the soil can be classified as sandy, clayey and loamy. | |
| (iii) Teacher will tell that the size of the particles in a soil have a very important influence on its properties. Sand particles are quite large. They cannot fit closely together, so there are large spaces between them. These spaces are filled with air. We say that the sand is well aerated. Water can drain quickly through the spaces between the sand particles. So, sandy soils tend to be light, well aerated and rather dry. | (iii) Students will note it down in their notebooks. |
| (iv) Teacher will tell that the clay particles are much smaller. These particles are tightly packed together, leaving little space for air. Unlike sandy soil, water can be held in the tiny gaps between the particles of clay. Therefore, clay soils have little air. However, they are heavy as they hold more water than the sandy soils. | (iv) Students will note it down in their notebooks. |
| (v) Teacher will tell that the best topsoil for growing plants is loamy. Loamy soil is a mixture of sand, clay and another type of soil particle known as silt. Silt occurs as a deposit in riverbeds. The size of the silt particles is between those of sand and clay. The loamy soil also has humus in it. It has the right water holding capacity for the growth of plants. | (v) Students will note it down in their notebooks. |
| (vi) Teacher will tell that percolation is the movement of water through the soil. Measuring the percolation rate will help in determining that if the soil drains fast enough where we want to direct water with a downspout, create a swale or use retention grading. The percolation rate will also help to determine how suitable the soil is for certain trees. Some need well-drained soil while others prefer a waterlogged site. Percolation rate of water is different in | (vi) Students will note it down in their notebooks. |

| | |
|---|---|
| different types of soil. It is the highest in the sandy soil and least in the clayey soil. To calculate the percolation rate, we use the formula as follows: $\text{percolation rate (ml/min.)} = \frac{\text{amount of water (ml)}}{\text{percolation time (min.)}}$ | |

**(8) Experiment**

| Activity | Discussion | Result |
|---|---|---|
| Collect samples of clayey, loamy and sandy soils. Take a fistful of soil from one of the samples. Remove any pebbles, rocks or grass blades from it. Now add water drop by drop and knead the soil. Add just enough water so that a ball can be made from it, but at the same time, it should not be sticky. Try to make a ball from this soil. On a flat surface, roll this ball into a cylinder. Try to make a ring from this cylinder. Repeat this activity with other samples also. | Does the extent to which a soil can be shaped indicate its type?<br>Can you suggest which type of soil would be the best for making pots, toys and statues? | The clayey soil would be the best for making pots, toys and statues. |
| | For another activity, divide yourself into three teams. Name the teams A, B and C. You will find out how fast the water passes down the soil. You will need a hollow cylinder or a | |

| | | |
|---|---|---|
| | pipe. Ensure that each team uses pipes of the same diameter. Some suggestions for obtaining such a pipe are given below:<br>(1) If possible, get a small tin can and cut off its bottom.<br>(2) If PVC pipe (approx. diameter 5 cm) is available, cut it into 20 cm long pieces and use them. | |
| At the place where you collect the soil, place the pipe about 2 cm deep in the ground. Pour 200 ml water in the pipe slowly. For measuring 200 ml water, you can use any empty 200 ml bottle. Note the time when you start pouring water. When all the water has percolated leaving the pipe empty, note the time again. | Be careful not to let the water spill over or run down on the outside of the pipe while pouring. Calculate the rate of percolation by using the following formula:<br>$\text{percolation rate (ml/min.)} = \frac{\text{amount of water (ml)}}{\text{percolation time (min.)}}$ | For example, suppose that for a certain sample, it took 20 minutes for 200 ml to percolate. So,<br>$\text{rate of percolation} = \frac{200\text{ml}}{20\text{ min}} = 10\text{ml/min}$ |

**(9) Recapitulation**

(1) Tick the most suitable answer in questions (a) and (b).

(a) The water holding capacity is the highest in

(i) sandy soil (ii) clayey soil

(iii) loamy soil (iv) mixture of sand and loamy

(b) In addition to the rock particles, the soil contains

(i) air and water

(ii) water and plants

(iii) minerals, organic matter, air and water

(iv) water, air and plants

(2) Match the items in Column I with those in Column II:

| Column I | Column II |
|---|---|
| (i) A home for living organisms | (a) Large particles |
| (ii) Upper layer of the soil | (b) All kinds of soil |
| (iii) Sandy soil | (c) Dark in colour |
| (iv) Middle layer of the soil | (d) Small particles and packed tight |
| (v) Clayey soil | (e) Lesser amount of humus |

**(10) Homework**

- Explain how soil is formed?
- How is clayey soil useful for crops?
- List the differences between clayey soil and sandy soil.

**THE BEST TEACHERS BECOME THE BEST TEACHERS BY BEING THEIR OWN BEST STUDENTS.**

**— Laurie Gray**

# LESSON PLAN – 5

| **Subject:** Science | **Date:** ________ |
|---|---|
| **Topic:** Breathing | **Duration:** 35 – 40 minutes |
| | **Class:** 7th |

**(1) General Objectives**

- To develop the interest of students in learning science.
- To develop the abilities of imagination, reasoning and observation.
- To inculcate creativity in students.
- To develop the understanding about the reality and observation.
- To enable them to get knowledge contained in the lesson.

**(2) Specific Objectives**

- To enable the students to know about breathing.
- To enable the students to describe the process of inhalation and exhalation.
- To enable the students to know about breathing rate.
- To enable the students to observe the changes in breathing rates under different conditions.
- To enable the students to notice that when they released their breath after holding it for some seconds, they will have to be breathe heavily.

**(3) Previous Knowledge**

The students must have at least general familiarities with respiration, cellular respiration, aerobic respiration, anaerobic respiration, etc.

**(4) Teaching Aids**

Blackboard, chalk, duster, pointer, models, etc.

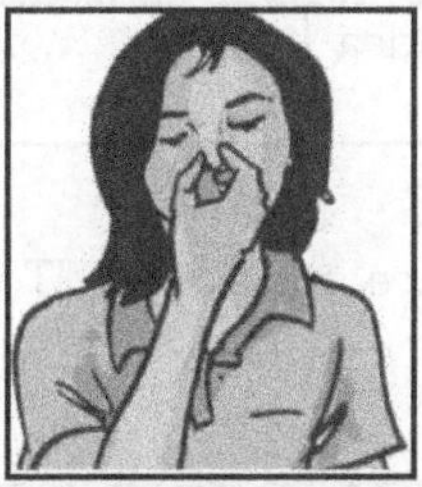

Fig. 3.10: Holding Breadth

Table 3.3

| Name of the classmate | Breathing rate | | | |
|---|---|---|---|---|
| | Normal | After a brisk walk for 10 minutes | After running fast 100 m | At rest |
| Shankar | 14 – 16 | 18 – 20 | 24 – 26 | 14 – 16 |
| Santosh | 13 – 15 | 17 – 20 | 23 – 26 | 13 – 15 |
| Shiva | 14 –17 | 18 – 21 | 24 – 27 | 14 – 17 |
| Sita | 15 – 17 | 19 – 21 | 25 – 27 | 15 – 17 |
| Kirti | 12 – 14 | 16 – 18 | 21 – 23 | 12 – 14 |

**(5) Introduction**

| Teacher's Question | Student's Answer |
|---|---|
| (i) Why do we respire? | (i) We respire to get energy from food or to live. |
| (ii) Give the definition of respiration. | (ii) It is a process by which organisms exchange gases, especially oxygen and carbon dioxide, with the environment. |
| (iii) What do you know about cellular respiration? | (iii) The process of breakdown of food in the cell with the release of energy is called cellular respiration. |
| (iv) Define aerobic and anaerobic respiration. | (iv) Breakdown of glucose with the use of oxygen is called aerobic respiration. Breakdown of food without the use of oxygen is called anaerobic respiration. |
| (v) Are there organisms that can survive in the absence of air? | (v) Yes, like yeast, tetanus, etc. |
| (vi) Explain the process of breathing. | (vi) ........................ |

| (vii) Do you have any idea about inhaling or exhaling? | (vii) ...................... |
|---|---|

### (6) Statement of topic

Now, teacher will announce the topic, "Today, we will study about breathing process."

### (7) Presentation

| Teacher's Action | Student's Activity |
|---|---|
| (i) Teacher will tell all the students that breathing is the process that moves air in and out of the lungs. Aerobic organisms of these types such as birds, mammals and reptiles require oxygen to release energy via respiration, in the form of the metabolism of energy-rich molecules such as glucose. Breathing is only one process that delivers oxygen to where it is needed in the body and removes carbon dioxide. | (i) After listening the teacher, students will note it down in their notebooks. |
| (ii) Teacher will tell that taking in of air rich in oxygen into the body is called inhalation and giving out of air rich in carbon dioxide is known as exhalation. It is a continuous process, which goes on all the time and throughout the life of an organism. | (ii) Students will note it down in their notebooks. |
| (iii) Teacher will tell that the number of times a person breathes in a minute is termed as the breathing rate. Both inhalation and exhalation take place. A breath means one inhalation plus one exhalation | (iii) Students will note it down in their notebooks. Some students ask about what is normal breathing rate. |
| (iv) Teacher will tell that on an average, an adult human being at rest breathes in and out 15–18 times in a minute. During heavy exercise, the breathing rate can increase upto 25 times per minute. While we exercise, not only do we breathe fast, we also take deep breaths, and thus, inhale more oxygen. | (iv) Students will note it down in their notebooks. |

**(8) Experiment**

| Activity | Discussion | Result |
|---|---|---|
| Close your nostrils and mouth tightly, and look at a watch. | What did you feel after some time? | We felt suffocation, which means that we cannot live without breathing. |
| Note down the time for which you could hold your breath. | How long were you able to keep both of them closed? | 15 breaths/min (app.) |
| Record your breathing rate as soon as you finish and also after complete rest. | Tabulate your findings and compare your breathing rates under different conditions with those of your classmates. | See in table 3.3 |

**(9) Recapitulation**

- Why does an athlete breathe faster and deeper than usual after finishing the race?
- List the similarities and differences between aerobic and anaerobic respiration.

**(10) Homework**

(a) Mark 'T' if the statement is true and 'F' if it is false:

(i) During heavy exercise, the breathing rate of a person slows down. (T/F)

(ii) Plants carry out photosynthesis only during the day and respiration only at night. (T/F)

(iii) Frogs breathe through their skins as well as their lungs. (T/F)

(iv) The fishes have lungs for respiration. (T/F)

(v) The size of the chest cavity increases during inhalation. (T/F)

(b) Visit a doctor. Find out about artificial respiration. Ask the doctor:

(i) When does a person need artificial respiration?

(ii) Does the person need to be kept on artificial respiration temporarily or permanently?

(iii) From where can the person get supply of oxygen for artificial respiration?

(c) Measure the breathing rate of the members of your family and some of your friends. Investigate:

(i) If the breathing rate of children is different from that of adults.

(ii) If the breathing rate of males is different from that of females.

**IT IS THE SUPREME ART OF THE TEACHER TO AWAKEN JOY IN CREATIVE EXPRESSION AND KNOWLEDGE.**

**— Albert Einstein**

# LESSON PLAN – 6

| | |
|---|---|
| **Subject:** Science | **Date:** _______ |
| **Topic:** Reproduction in plants | **Duration:** 35 – 40 minutes |
| | **Class:** 7th |

## (1) General Objectives

- To develop the interest of students in learning science.
- To develop the abilities of imagination, reasoning and observation.
- To inculcate creativity in students.
- To develop the understanding about the reality and observation.
- To enable them to get knowledge contained in the lesson.

## (2) Specific Objectives

- To enable the students to know how plants reproduce.
- To enable the students to describe modes of reproduction in plants.
- To enable the students to learn about asexual reproduction.
- To enable the students to learn reproduction in plants by vegetative propagation.
- To enable the students to observe methods of asexual reproduction.

## (3) Previous Knowledge

The students must have at least general familiarities with reproduction, herbs, shrubs, trees, leaf, roots, flower, etc.

## (4) Teaching Aids

Blackboard, chalk, duster, pointer, models, rose, potato, money plants, magnifying glass, ginger, Bryophyllum (sprout leaf plant), other useful equipments, etc.

**Fig. 3.11: Stem cutting of rose**

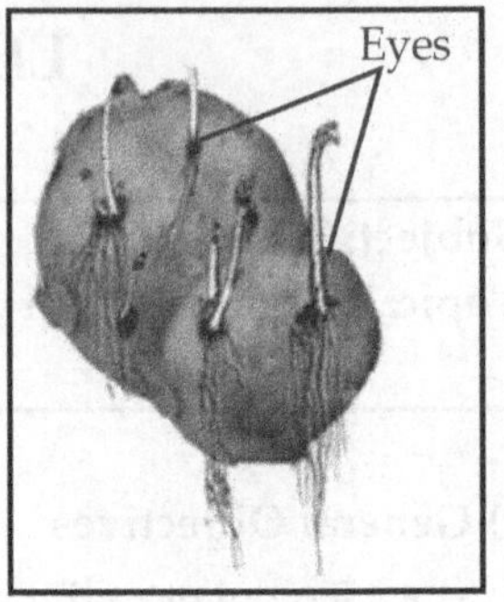

**Fig. 3.12: Potato plant sprouting from an eye**

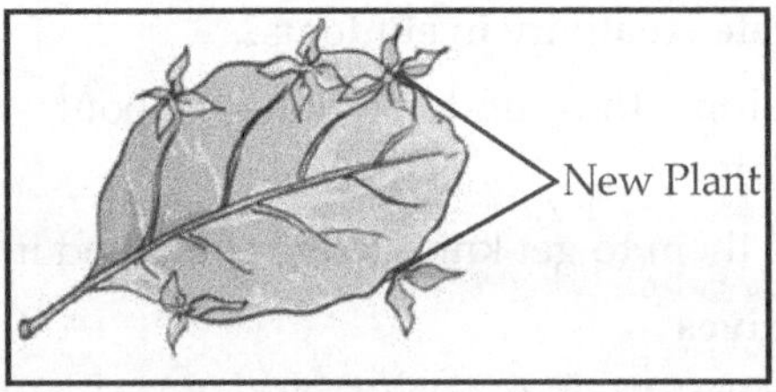

**Fig. 3.13: Leaf of Bryophyllum with buds in the margin**

### (5) Introduction

| Teacher's Question | Student's Answer |
|---|---|
| (i) What do you know about reproduction? | (i) It is the biological process by which new "offspring" individual organisms are produced from their "parents". |
| (ii) What do you know about plants? | (ii) Plants are usually grouped into herbs, shrubs, trees and climbers based on their height, stems and branches. |
| (iii) Explain herbs. | (iii) A soft-stem flowering plant, which generally dies back at the end of each growing season are called herbs. |
| (iv) Explain shrubs. | (iv) A woody plant of relatively low height, having several stems arising from the base and lacking a single trunk are called shrubs. |
| (v) Explain trees. | (v) A plant having a permanent woody main stem or trunk grows ordinarily to a considerable height and usually developing branches at some distance from the ground are called trees. |

| | |
|---|---|
| (vi) What do you know about a leaf? | (vi) A leaf is functioning as a principal organ of photosynthesis and transpiration in most plants. |
| (vii) What do you know about roots? | (vii) Roots develop from the radicles and grow downwards into the soil, anchoring the plants and absorbing nutrients and moisture. |
| (viii) Give definition and examples of some flowers. | (viii) The reproductive structure of some seed-bearing plants is called a flower. For example sunflower, tulips, marigold, etc. |
| (ix) How do plants reproduce? | (ix) .............................. |

**(6) Statement of topic**

Now, teacher will announce the topic, "Today, we will study about reproduction in plants."

**(7) Presentation**

| Teacher's Action | Student's Activity |
|---|---|
| (i) Teacher will tell all the students that the roots, stems and leaves are called the vegetative parts of a plant. After a certain period of growth, most plants bear flowers. You may have seen the mango trees flowering in spring. The flowers that give rise to juicy mango fruit we enjoy in summer. We eat the fruits and usually discard the seeds. Seeds germinate and form new plants. | (i) After listening the teacher, students will note it down in their notebooks. Some students may ask that what the functions of flowers in plants be. |
| (ii) Teacher will tell that the flowers perform the functions of reproduction in plants. Flowers are the reproductive parts of a plant. A flower may have either the male part or the female part or both male and female parts. | (ii) Students will note it down in their notebooks. |
| (iii) Teacher will tell that there are several ways, which help plants in reproducing their offspring. These are categorised into two types: (i) asexual and (ii) sexual reproduction. | (iii) Students will note it down in their notebooks. Students thought that new plants always grow from seeds. However, they have never seen the seeds of sugarcane, potato |

| | |
|---|---|
| | and rose. They want to know how these plants reproduce. |
| (iv) Teacher will tell that in asexual reproduction plants can give rise to new plants without seeds, whereas in sexual reproduction, new plants are obtained from seeds. | (iv) Students will note it down in their notebooks. |
| (v) Teacher will tell that vegetative propagation is a type of asexual reproduction in which new plants are produced from vegetative reproduction parts, i.e. roots, stems, leaves and buds. | (v) Students will note it down in their notebooks. |

**(8) Experiment**

| Activity | Discussion | Result |
|---|---|---|
| Cut a branch of rose or champa with a node. Bury the cutting in the soil. A node is a part of the stem/branch at which a leaf arises. | This piece of branch is termed as cutting. | |
| Water the cutting every day and observe its growth. | Observe and record the number of days taken for roots to come out and new leaves to arise. | |
| Try the same activity by growing money plant in a jar of water. | Record your observations. | You must have seen flower buds developing into flowers. Apart from flower buds, there are buds in the axil (point of attachment of the leaf at the node) of leaves, which develop into shoots. |
| | These buds are called vegetative buds. A bud consists of a short stem around which immature | |

| | | |
|---|---|---|
| | overlapping leaves are folded. The vegetative buds can also give rise to new plants. | |
| Take a fresh potato. Observe the scars on it with the help of a magnifying glass. | You may find bud(s) in them. These scars are also called "eyes." | |
| Cut a few pieces of a potato, each with an eye and bury them in the soil. Water the pieces regularly for a few days. | Observe their progress. | We will found that ginger with new plants sprouting from it. |
| | Likewise, you can also grow ginger or turmeric. Bryophyllum (sprout leaf plant) has buds in the margins of leaves. If a leaf of this plant falls on a moist soil, each bud can give rise to a new plant. | |

**(9) Recapitulation**

(a) Fill in the blanks:

(i) Production of new individuals from the vegetative part of parent is called _______.

(ii) A flower may have either male or female reproductive parts. Such a flower is called _______.

(b) Tick ( √ ) the correct answer:

(i) The reproductive part of a plant is the (i) leaf (ii) stem (iii) root (iv) flower

(ii) Bryophyllum can reproduce by its (i) stem (ii) leaves (iii) roots (iv) all of these

(c) Describe the different methods of asexual reproduction. Give examples.

**(10) Homework**

- State the main difference between asexual and sexual reproduction.
- Sketch the reproductive parts of a flower.

> **A GOOD TEACHER CAN INSPIRE HOPE, IGNITE THE IMAGINATION, AND INSTILL A LOVE OF LEARNING**
>
> **— Brad Henry**

# LESSON PLAN — 7

| | |
|---|---|
| **Subject:** Science | **Date:** ________ |
| **Topic:** Commercial use of microorganisms | **Duration:** 35 – 40 minutes |
| | **Class:** 8th |

**(1) General Objectives**

- To develop the interest of students in learning science.
- To develop the abilities of imagination, reasoning and observation.
- To inculcate creativity in students.
- To develop the understanding about the reality and observation.
- To enable them to get knowledge contained in the lesson.

**(2) Specific Objectives**

- To enable the students to know about commercial uses of microorganisms.
- To enable the students to know about fermentation.

**(3) Previous Knowledge**

The students must have at least general familiarities with microorganisms or microbes, its major groups, its presence, i.e. where do microorganisms live, diseases caused by them, its general uses, etc.

**(4) Teaching Aids**

Blackboard, chalk, duster, pointer, models of microorganisms, water, sugar, 500ml beaker, teaspoons, yeast powder and other useful equipments.

**(5) Introduction**

| Teacher's Question | Student's Answer |
|---|---|
| (i) What do you know about microorganisms or microbes? | (i) Organisms, which are too small to be seen with naked eyes but visible under a microscope are called microorganisms or microbes. |
| (ii) What are the major groups of microorganisms? | (ii) Microorganisms are classified into four major groups, i.e. bacteria, fungi, protozoa and some algae. |

| | |
|---|---|
| (iii) What are the diseases caused by microorganisms? | (iii) Chicken pox, Common cold, Diarrheal diseases, Malaria, Skin diseases, etc. are some common diseases caused by microorganisms. |
| (iv) Give some uses of microorganisms. | (iv) Used in the preparation of curd, bread and cake, cleaning up of the environment, preparation of medicines, increase soil fertility by fixing nitrogen, etc. |
| (v) What are the commercial uses of microorganisms? | (v) ........................ |

**(6) Statement of topic**

Now, teacher will announce the topic, "Today, we will study about commercial uses of microorganisms."

**(7) Presentation**

| Teacher's Action | Student's Activity |
|---|---|
| (i) Teacher will tell all the students without microbes, there would be no fertile soil to grow vegetables and flowers, no bread or cheese and no beer or wine! Long ago, before people were able to see microbes under microscopes or even knew that they existed, human societies began learning how to put them to use. | (ii) After listening the teacher, students will note it down in their notebooks. |
| (iii) Teacher will tell that commercial use of microorganisms, called biotechnology, has been revolutionised through the advent of genetic engineering, which has shown great potential for medical use. For example, many people cannot digest the sugar present in raw milk (lactose). When animals were domesticated about 10,000 years ago, people learned how to use bacteria to digest raw milk from domesticated animals and turn it into yogurt and cheese, which are more palatable. An entire dairy industry was | (ii) Students will note it down in their notebooks. |

| | |
|---|---|
| born from bacteria. | |
| (iii)Teacher will tell that humans also learned how to use yeast, another kind of microbe, to digest the sugars in fruit such as grapes, into alcohol to make wine. Yeast also digests sugars in grains like barley malt to make alcohol in beers. Some experts think that the ancient Egyptians developed grain and yeast to make beer even before they used it to make bread. The tablet, from Nippur in Iraq, contains prescriptions for salves and internal remedies. Most of the medicines are to be taken with beer. | (iii) Students will note it down in their notebooks. |

**(8) Experiment**

| Activity | Discussion | Result |
|---|---|---|
| Take a 500 ml beaker filled upto ¾ with water. Dissolve 2-3 teaspoons of sugar in it. Add half a spoon of yeast powder to the sugar solution. Keep it covered in a warm place for 4-5 hours. Now smell the solution. | Could you get a smell? | Yes, this is the smell of alcohol as sugar has been converted into alcohol by yeast. This process of conversion of sugar into alcohol is known as fermentation. |

**(9) Recapitulation**

(a) Fill in the blanks:

(i) Microorganisms can be seen with the help of a _______.

(ii) Alcohol is produced with the help of _______.

(iii) Cholera is caused by _______.

(b) Tick the correct answer:

(i) Yeast is used in the production of:

• sugar • alcohol • hydrochloric acid • oxygen

(ii) The most common carrier of communicable diseases is:

• ant • housefly • dragonfly • spider

(iii) The bread or idli dough rises because of

• heat • grinding • growth of yeast cells • kneading

(iv) The process of conversion of sugar into alcohol is called

- nitrogen fixation
- moulding
- fermentation
- infection

(c) Can microorganisms be seen with the naked eye? If not, how can they be seen?

**(10) Homework**

- Write 10 lines on the usefulness of microorganisms in our lives.
- Write a short paragraph on the harms caused by microorganisms.

**YOUR BEST TEACHER IS YOUR LAST MISTAKE.**

— **Ralph Nader**

# LESSON PLAN – 8

| | |
|---|---|
| **Subject:** Science | **Date:** ________ |
| **Topic:** Types of synthetic fibres | **Duration:** 35 – 40 minutes |
| | **Class:** 8th |

**(1) General Objectives**

- To develop the interest of students in learning science.
- To develop the abilities of imagination, reasoning and observation.
- To inculcate creativity in students.
- To develop the understanding about the reality and observation.
- To enable them to get knowledge contained in the lesson.

**(2) Specific Objectives**

- To enable the students to know about different types of fibres.
- To enable the students to learn about rayon, its characteristics and its uses.
- To enable the students to learn about nylon, its characteristics and its uses
- To enable the students to know about Polyester and Acrylic.

**(3) Previous Knowledge**

The students must have at least general familiarities with natural and artificial fibres, synthetic fibre, polymer, etc.

**(4) Teaching Aids**

Blackboard, chalk, duster, pointer, iron stand with a clamp, cotton thread of about 60 cm length, weights and other equipments, etc.

**Table 3.4**

| S.No. | Type of thread/fibre | Total weight required to break the thread |
|---|---|---|
| (1) | Cotton | 75g |
| (2) | Wool | 750g |
| (3) | Silk | 150g |
| (4) | Nylon | 375g |

**(5) Introduction**

| Teacher's Question | Student's Answer |
|---|---|
| (i) What do you know about natural fibres? | (i) These are bio-based fibres or fibres from vegetable and animal origin. |
| (ii) What do you know about artificial fibres? | (ii) These are threadlike materials invented by human researchers. Such fibres do not exist naturally. |
| (iii) Try to recall the uniform pattern found in a necklace of beads joined with the help of a thread or, try to join a number of paper clips together to make a long chain. Is there any similarity between the two? | (iii) Yes, a synthetic fibre is a chain of small units joined together and when these units combine to form a large single unit is known as a polymer. |
| (iv) Well good, do you know where the word polymer comes from? | (iv) Yes, it comes from two Greek words, 'poly' meaning many and 'mer' meaning part/unit. So, a poly-mer is made of many repeating units. |
| (v) Very good, now tell me briefly about types of synthetic fibres. | (v) .................. |

**(6) Statement of topic**

Now, teacher will announce the topic, "Today, we will know about types of synthetic fibres."

**(7) Presentation**

| Teacher's Action | Student's Activity |
|---|---|
| (i) Teacher will tell all the students that depending upon the types of chemicals used for manufacturing synthetic fibres, they are named as Rayon, Nylon, Polyester and Acrylic. | (i) After listening teacher, students will note it down in their notebooks. |
| (ii) Teacher will tell that towards the end of the nineteenth century, scientists were successful in obtaining a fibre having properties similar to that of silk. Such a fibre | (ii) Students will note it down in their notebooks. |

| | |
|---|---|
| was obtained by chemical treatment of wood pulp. This fibre was called rayon or artificial silk. Although rayon is obtained from a natural source, wood pulp, yet it is a man-made fibre. It is cheaper than silk and can be woven like silk fibres. It can also be dyed in a wide variety of colours. Rayon is mixed with cotton to make bed sheets or mixed with wool to make carpets. | |
| (iii) Teacher will tell that nylon is another man-made fibre. In 1931, it was made without using any natural raw material (from plant or animal). It was prepared from coal, water and air. It was the first fully synthetic fibre. Nylon fibre was strong, elastic and light. It was lustrous and easy to wash. So, it became very popular for making clothes. We use many articles made from nylon, such as socks, ropes, tents, toothbrushes, car seat belts, sleeping bags, curtains, etc. Nylon is also used for making parachutes and ropes for rock climbing. | (iii) Students will note it down in their notebooks.<br>Some students ask is nylon fibre really so strong that we can make nylon parachutes and ropes for rock climbing. |
| (iv) Teacher will tell that a nylon thread is actually stronger than a steel wire. | (iv) Students will note it down in their notebooks. |
| (v) Teacher will tell that polyester is another synthetic fibre. Fabric made from this fibre does not get wrinkled easily. It remains crisp and is easy to wash. Therefore, it is quite suitable for making dress material. You must have seen people wearing nice polyester shirts and other dresses. Terylene is a popular polyester. It can be | (v) Students will note it down in their notebooks.<br>A student says my mother always buys PET bottles and PET jars for storing rice and sugar. I wonder what PET is! |

| | |
|---|---|
| drawn into very fine fibres that can be woven like any other yarn. | |
| (vi)Teacher will tell that PET is a very familiar form of polyester. It is used for making bottles, utensils, films, wires and many other useful products. | (v) Students will note it down in their notebooks. |
| (vii) Teacher will tell that we wear sweaters and use shawls or blankets in the winter. Many of these are actually not made from natural wool, though they appear to resemble wool. These are prepared from another type of synthetic fibre called acrylic. The wool obtained from natural sources is quite expensive, whereas clothes made from acrylic are relatively cheap. They are available in a variety of colours. | (vi) Students will note it down in their notebooks. |
| (vii) Teacher will tell that synthetic fibres are more durable and affordable, which makes them more popular than natural fibres. | (vii) Students will note it down in their notebooks. |

**(8) Experiment**

| Activity | Discussion | Result |
|---|---|---|
| Take an iron stand with a clamp. Tie a cotton thread of about 60 cm length to the clamp so that it hangs freely from it. At the free end, suspend a pan so that weights can be placed in it. Add weights one by one till the thread breaks. | Note down the total weight required to break the thread. This weight indicates the strength of the fibre. Repeat the same ac-tivity with threads of wool, silk and nylon. Tabulate the data as shown in Table 3.4. Arrange the threads in order of their increasing strength. | Different types of threads made of different synthetic fibres need different weights to break the thread. |

**(9) Recapitulation**

(a) Explain why some fibres are called synthetic.

(b) Mark (✓) the correct answer:

Rayon is different from synthetic fibres because:

(i) it has a silk like appearance

(ii) it is obtained from wood pulp

(iii) its fibres can also be woven like those of natural fibres

(c) Give examples, which indicate that nylon fibres are very strong.

**(10) Homework**

- Santosh wants to buy shirts for summer. Should he buy cotton shirts or shirts made from synthetic material? Advise Santosh, giving your reason.
- 'Manufacturing synthetic fibres is actually helping conservation of forests'. Comment.
- Visit five families in your neighbourhood and enquire about the kind of clothes they use, the reason for their choice and advantages of using them in terms of cost, durability and maintenance. Make a short report and submit it to your teacher.

**A GOOD TEACHER MUST KNOW THE RULES; A GOOD PUPIL, THE EXCEPTIONS.**

**– Martin H. Fischer**

# LESSON PLAN – 9

| **Subject:** Science | **Date:** ________ |
|---|---|
| **Topic:** Combustion | **Duration:** 35 – 40 minutes |
| | **Class:** 8th |

## (1) General Objectives

- To develop the interest of students in learning science.
- To develop the abilities of imagination, reasoning and observation.
- To inculcate creativity in students.
- To develop the understanding about the reality and observation.
- To enable them to get knowledge contained in the lesson.

## (2) Specific Objectives

- To enable the students to learn about combustion.
- To enable the students to learn about combustible and non-combustible substances.
- To enable the students to show that air is essential for burning.

## (3) Previous Knowledge

The students must have at least general familiarities with different kinds of fuel for various purposes, burning of a candle, difference between the burning of a candle and the burning of a fuel like coal, flame, etc.

## (4) Teaching Aids

Blackboard, chalk, duster, pointer, table, candle, glass chimney, wooden blocks and other equipments.

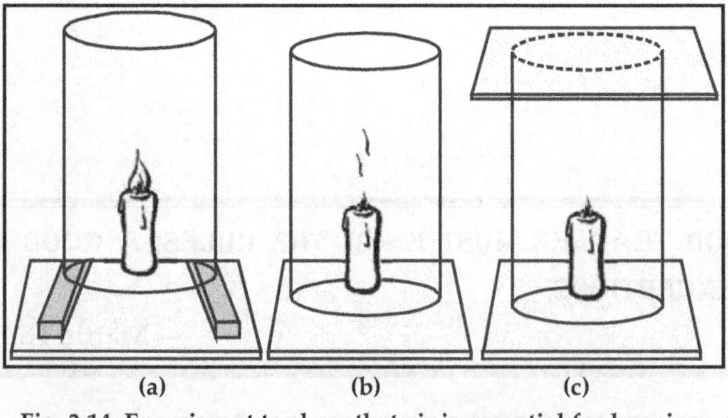

(a) (b) (c)

**Fig. 3.14: Experiment to show that air is essential for burning**

**(5) Introduction**

| Teacher's Question | Student's Answer |
|---|---|
| (i) What do you know about fuel? | (i) Any inflammable substance. |
| (ii) Can you name a few fuels used in our homes? | (ii) Fuels like wood, coal, kerosene, domestic gas, cow dung, etc. are used in our homes for cooking. |
| (iii) What fuels are used for running automobiles? | (iii) Fuels like petrol, diesel, compressed natural gas (CNG), etc. are used for running automobiles. |
| (iv) Are you familiar with burning of a candle? | (iv) Yes sir. |
| (v) Good, what is the difference between the burning of a candle and the burning of a fuel like coal? | (v) Candle burns with a flame whereas coal does not. |
| (vi) Well, now tell me about flame. | (vi) Flame can be defined as the zone of burning gases and fine suspended matter associated with rapid combustion; a hot, glowing mass of burning gas or vapour. |
| (vii) What do you know about combustion? | (vii) .................... |

**(6) Statement of topic**

Now, teacher will announce the topic, "Today, we will study about combustion."

**(7) Presentation**

| Teacher's Action | Student's Activity |
|---|---|
| (i) Teacher will tell all the students that magnesium burns to form magnesium oxide and produces heat and light. | (i) After listening teacher, students will note it down in their note-books. |
| (ii) Teacher will tell that a chemical process in which a substance reacts with oxygen to give off heat is called combustion. | (ii) Students will note it down in their notebooks. |
| (iii) Teacher will tell that the substance that undergoes combus-tion is said to be combustible. It is | (iii) Students will note it down in their notebooks. |

| | |
|---|---|
| also called a fuel. The fuel may be solid, liquid or gas. Sometimes, light is also given off during combustion, either as a flame or as a glow. | |
| (iv) Teacher will tell all the students that the word non-combustible can be used for a kind of substance that cannot be burnt easily. For example, stone, plaster-board, fibreglass/glass, asbestos, steel, metal, etc. | (iv) Students will note it down into their notebooks. |

**(8) Experiment**

| Activity | Discussion | Result |
|---|---|---|
| Fix a lighted candle on a table. Put a glass chimney over the candle and rest it on a few wooden blocks in such a way that air can enter the chimney. | Observe what happens to the flame. | |
| Now remove the blocks and let the chimney rest on the table. | Again, observe the flame. | |
| Finally, put a glass plate over the chimney. | Watch the flame again. What happens in the three cases? Does the flame flicker off? Does it flicker and give smoke? Does it burn unaffected? Can you infer anything at all about the role played by air in the process of burning? | We find that for combustion, air is necessary. The candle burns freely incase (a) when air can enter the chimney from below. In case (b), when air does not enter the chimney from below, the flame flickers and produces smoke. In case (c), the flame finally goes off |

| | | because the air is not available. |
|---|---|---|

**(9) Recapitulation**

(a) List conditions under which combustion can take place.

(b) Fill in the blanks:

(i) Burning of wood and coal causes _______ of air.

(ii) A liquid fuel, used in homes is _______.

(c) Give reasons:

(i) Water is not used to control fires involving electrical equipment.

(ii) LPG is a better domestic fuel than wood.

(iii) Paper by itself catches fire easily whereas a piece of paper wrapped around an aluminium pipe does not.

**(10) Homework**

- Make a labelled diagram of a candle flame.
- Name the unit in which the calorific value of a fuel is expressed.

**I'VE LEARNED THAT MISTAKES CAN OFTEN BE AS GOOD A TEACHER AS SUCCESS.**

— **Jack Welch**

# LESSON PLAN — 10

| | |
|---|---|
| **Subject:** Science | **Date:** ______ |
| **Topic:** Asexual reproduction in Animals | **Duration:** 35 – 40 minutes |
| | **Class:** 8th |

**(1) General Objectives**

- To develop the interest of students in learning science.
- To develop the abilities of imagination, reasoning and observation.
- To inculcate creativity in students.
- To develop the understanding about the reality and observation.
- To enable them to get knowledge contained in the lesson.

**(2) Specific Objectives**

- To enable the students to learn about modes of reproduction in animals.
- To enable the students to learn about asexual reproduction in animals.
- To enable the students to learn about budding in hydra.
- To enable the students to know about how very small animals like hydra and microscopic organism like amoeba reproduce?
- To enable the students to learn about binary fission in amoeba.

**(3) Previous Knowledge**

The students must have at least general familiarities with reproduction, its different modes, reproduction in plants, etc.

**(4) Teaching Aids**

Blackboard, chalk, duster, pointer, models and figures of asexual reproduction in animals, slides of hydra, microscope, etc.

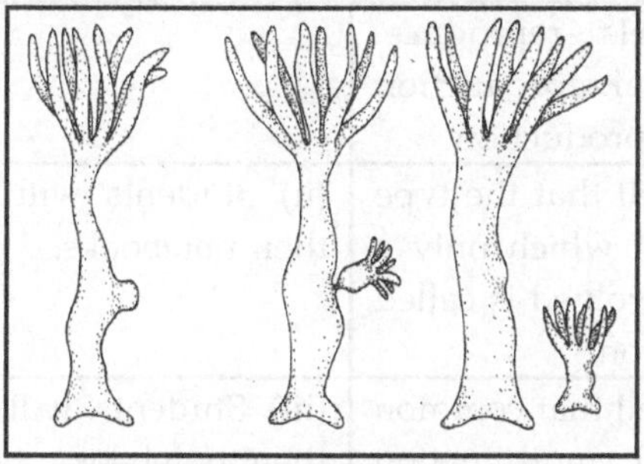

**Fig. 3.15: Budding in Hydra**

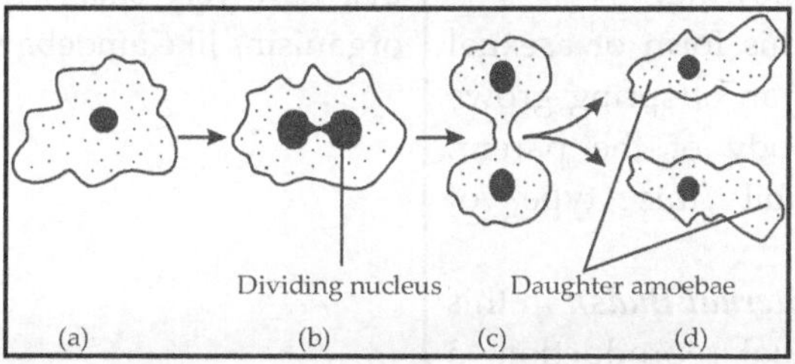


**Fig. 3.16: Binary fission in Amoeba**

**(5) Introduction**

| Teacher's Question | Student's Answer |
|---|---|
| (i) What do you know about reproduction? | (i) It is a process in which new "offspring" individual organisms are produced from their "parents". |
| (ii) What do you know about reproduction in plants? | (ii) It is the production of new individuals or offspring in plants, which can be accomplished by sexual or asexual means. |
| (iii) Good, tell about modes of reproduction in animals. | (iii) .......................... |
| (iv) Do you have any idea about asexual reproduction in animals? | (iv) .......................... |

**(6) Statement of topic**

Now, teacher will announce the topic, "Today, we will study about asexual reproduction in animals."

**(7) Presentation**

| Teacher's Action | Student's Activity |
|---|---|
| (i) Teacher will tell all the students that there are two modes | (i) After listening teacher, students will note it down in their notebooks. |

| | |
|---|---|
| by which animals reproduce. These are: (a) Sexual reproduction and (b) Asexual reproduction. | |
| (ii) Teacher will tell that the type of reproduction in which only a single parent is involved is called asexual reproduction. | (ii) Students will note it down in their notebooks. |
| (iii) Teacher will tell that common forms of asexual reproduction include the following:<br>***Budding:*** In this form of asexual reproduction, an offspring grows out of the body of the parent. Hydras exhibit this type of reproduction.<br>***Gemmules (Internal Buds):*** In this form of asexual reproduction, a parent releases a specialised mass of cells that can develop into offspring. Sponges exhibit this type of reproduction.<br>***Fragmentation:*** In this type of reproduction, the body of the parent breaks into distinct pieces, each of which can produce an offspring. Planarians exhibit this type of reproduction.<br>***Regeneration:*** In regeneration, if a piece of a parent is detached, it can grow and develop into a completely new individual. Echinoderms exhibit this type of reproduction.<br>***Parthenogenesis:*** This type of reproduction involves the development of an egg that has not been fertilised into an individual. Animals like most kinds of wasps, bees and ants that have no sex chromosomes | (iii) Students will note it down in their notebooks. Some students ask that how very small and microscopic organisms like amoeba reproduce. |

| | |
|---|---|
| reproduce by this process. Some reptiles and fish are also capable of reproducing in this manner. | |
| (iv) Teacher will tell that amoeba is a single-celled organism. It begins the process of re-production by the division of its nucleus into two nuclei. This is followed by division of its body into two, each part receiving a nucleus. Finally, two amoebae are produced from one parent amoeba. This type of asexual reproduction in which an animal reproduces by dividing into two individuals is called binary fission. Apart from budding and binary fission, there are other methods by which a single parent reproduces the young ones. | (iv) Students will note it down in their notebooks. |

**(8) Experiment**

| Activity | Discussion | Result |
|---|---|---|
| (i) Get permanent slides of hydra, observe them using hand lens or a microscope. Look out for any bulges from the parent body. Count the number of bulges that you see in different slides. Also, note the size of the bulges. Draw the dia-gram of hydra, as you see it. | Do you see the buds? | In each hydra, there may be one or more bulges. These bulges are the developing new individuals and they are called buds. |

**(9) Recapitulation**

- Explain the importance of reproduction in organisms.
- Define asexual reproduction. Describe two methods of asexual reproduction in animals.

**(10) Homework**

Observe live hydra yourself and learn how they reproduce by performing the following activity:

During the summer months collect water weeds from ponds or ditches along with the pond water and put them in a glass jar. After a day or so you may see several hydra clinging to the sides of the jar.

Hydra is transparent, jelly-like and has tentacles. It clings to the jar with the base of its body. If the jar is shaken, the hydra will contract instantly into a small blob, at the same time drawing its tentacles in. Now take out few hydras from the jar and put them on a watch glass. Using a hand lens or a binocular or dissection microscope, observe the changes that are taking place in their body. Note down your observations.

**A TEACHER WHO IS ATTEMPTION TO TEACH WITHOUT INSPIRING THE PUPIL WITH A DESIRE TO LEARN IS HAMMERING ON COLD IRON.**

**— Horace Mann**

# LESSON PLAN — 11

| | |
|---|---|
| **Subject:** Science | **Date:** _______ |
| **Topic:** A Force can change the state of motion | **Duration:** 35 – 40 minute |
| | **Class:** 8th |

**(1) General Objectives**

- To develop the interest of students in learning science.
- To develop the abilities of imagination, reasoning and observation.
- To inculcate creativity in students.
- To develop the understanding about the reality and observation.
- To enable them to get knowledge contained in the lesson.

**(2) Specific Objectives**

- To enable the students to learn about what happens when a force acts on an object.
- To enable the students to observe that force applied on an object may change its speed.
- To enable the students to give the examples of situations in which applied force causes a change in the state of motion.

**(3) Previous Knowledge**

The students must have at least general familiarities with force, situations in which they push or pull to change the state of motion of objects, nature and interaction of forces, etc.

**(4) Teaching Aids**

Blackboard, chalk, duster, pointer, models and other activity related figures and objects, etc.

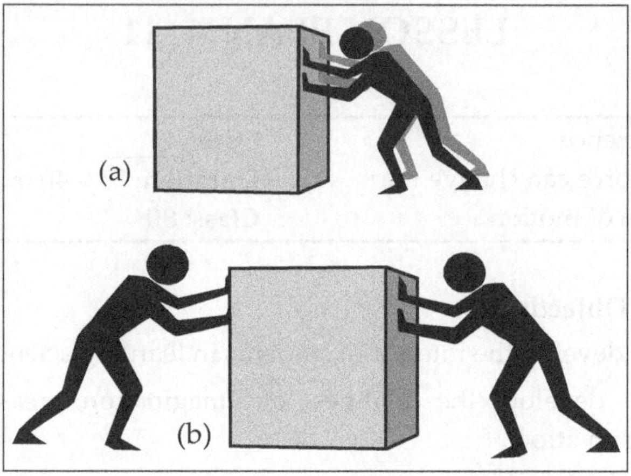


**Fig. 3.17: Two friends pushing a heavy load (a) in the same direction, (b) in opposite direction**

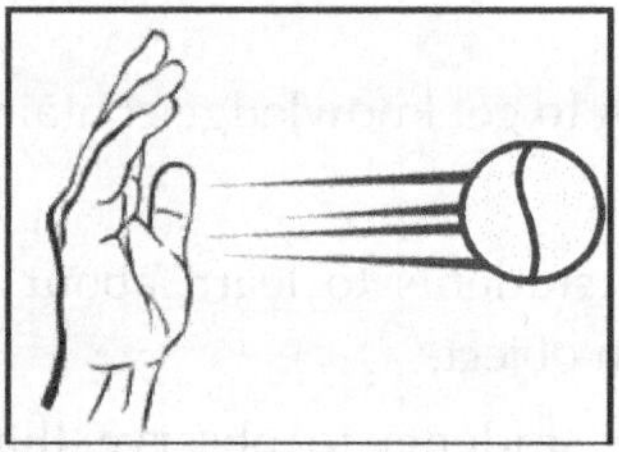

**(a)**

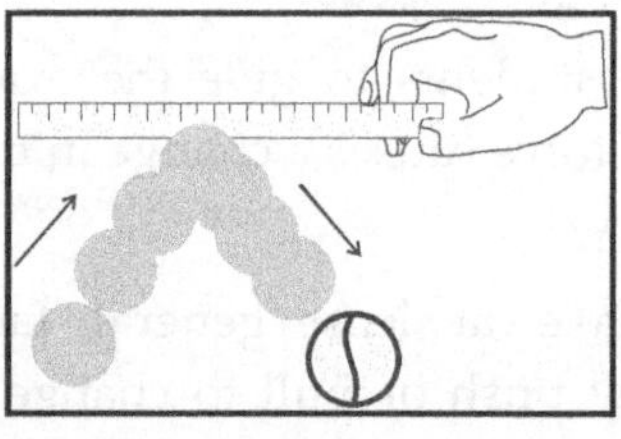

**(b)**

**Fig. 3.18: (a) A ball set in motion by pushing it along a level surface and (b) the direction of motion of the ball after it strikes the ruler placed in its path**

## (5) Introduction

| Teacher's Question | Student's Answer |
|---|---|
| (i) What do you know about force? | (i) It is a push or a pull on an object. |
| (ii) When does a force come into play? | (ii) When the interaction between two objects arises. |
| (iii) Moving a book placed on a | (iii) Push and pull. |

| | |
|---|---|
| table is which kind of action pushing, pulling, lifting or all of these? | |
| (iv) Well, what happens when a force acts on an object? | (iv) ........................ |

**(6) Statement of topic**

Now, teacher will announce the topic, "Today, we will study that what happens when a force acts on an object."

**(7) Presentation**

| Teacher's Action | Student's Activity |
|---|---|
| (i) Teacher will tell all the students that the state of motion of an object is described by its speed and the direction of motion. The state of rest is considered to be the state of zero speed. An object may be at rest or in motion; both are its states of motion. | (i) After listening teacher, students will note it down in their notebooks. |
| (ii) Teacher will tell that let us consider a situation; while taking a penalty kick in football, the player applies a force on the ball. Before being hit, the ball was at rest and therefore its speed was zero. The applied force makes the ball move towards the goal. Suppose, the goalkeeper dives or jumps up to save the goal. By his action, the goalkeeper tries to apply a force on the moving ball. The force applied by him can stop or deflect the ball, saving a goal being scored. If the goalkeeper succeeds in stopping the ball, its speed decreases to zero. These observations suggest that a force applied on an object may change its speed. If the force applied on the object is in the direction of its motion, the speed of the object increases. If the force is applied in the direction opposite to the direction of motion, then it results in a decrease in the speed of the object. | (ii) Students will note it down in their notebooks. |

| | |
|---|---|
| (ii) Teacher will tell that a change in either the speed of an object, or its direction of motion, or both, is described as a change in its state of motion. Thus, a force may bring a change in the state of motion of an object. | (ii) Students will note it down in their notebooks. Some students ask, does it mean that the application of force would always result in a change in the state of motion of the object. |
| (iii) Teacher will further say that a common experience is when force is applied to an object, does not result in any change in the state of motion. For example, a heavy box may not move at all even if you apply the maximum force that you can exert. Again, no effect of force is observed when you try to push a wall. | (iii) Students will note it down in their notebooks. |

**(8) Experiment**

| Activity | Discussion | Result |
|---|---|---|
| Take a rubber ball and place it on a level surface such as a tabletop or a concrete floor. Now, gently push the ball along the level surface. | Does the ball begin to move? | A ball at rest begins to move when a force is applied on it. |
| Take a ball and place it on a level surface as you did before. Make the ball move by giving it a push. Now place the ruler from your geometry box in its path. | In doing so, you would apply a force on the moving ball. Does the ball continue to move in the same direction after it strikes the ruler? | The ball deviates its path and moves in the other direction. |

**(9) Recapitulation**

- Give two examples each of situations in which you push or pull to change the state of motion of objects.
- Give two examples of situations in which applied force causes a change in the shape of an object.

**(10) Homework**

- A blacksmith hammers a hot piece of iron while making a tool. How does the force due to hammering affect the piece of iron?
- Name the forces acting on a plastic bucket containing water held above ground level in your hand. Discuss why the forces acting on the bucket do not bring a change in its state of motion.

**A TEACHER WHO IS ATTEMPTION TO TEACH WITHOUT INSPIRING THE PUPIL WITH A DESIRE TO LEARN IS HAMMERING ON COLD IRON.**

**— Horace Mann**

# LESSON PLAN — 12

| **Subject:** Science | **Date:** ______ |
|---|---|
| **Topic:** Sound produced by humans | **Duration:** 35 – 40 minutes |
| | **Class:** 8th |

## (1) General Objectives

- To develop the interest of students in learning science.
- To develop the abilities of imagination, reasoning and observation.
- To inculcate creativity in students.
- To develop the understanding about the reality and observation.
- To enable them to get knowledge contained in the lesson.

## (2) Specific Objectives

- To enable the students to learn about sounds produced by humans.
- To enable the students to learn about how the vocal cord functions.
- To enable the students to observe the reason why the voices of men, women and children are different.

## (3) Previous Knowledge

The students must have at least general familiarities with sound, its role, vibration, etc.

## (4) Teaching Aids

Blackboard, chalk, duster, pointer, models, rubber strips, a piece of paper, etc.

**Fig. 3.19: Plucking the rubber band**

**(5) Introduction**

| Teacher's Question | Student's Answer |
|---|---|
| (i) What do you know about sound? | (i) It is a wave that travels through air or water. |
| (ii) What is its importance? | It helps us to communicate with one another. In the music room of our school, we hear the sounds made by musical instruments like flute, tabla, harmonium, etc. |
| (iii) How is sound produced? | (iii) Sound is produced by vibrating objects. |
| (iv) What do you know about vibration? | (iv) The to and fro or back and forth motion of an object is termed as vibration. |
| (v) When we speak, does any part of our body vibrate? | (v) ...................... |

**(6) Statement of topic**

Now, teacher will announce the topic, "Today, we will study about sound produced by humans."

**(7) Presentation**

| Teacher's Action | Student's Activity |
|---|---|
| (i) Teacher will tell all the students that speak loudly for a while or sing a song or buzz like a bee. Put your hand on your throat. Do you feel any vibrations? | (i) .......................... |
| (ii) Teacher will tell that in humans, the sound is produced by the voice box or the larynx. Put your fingers on the throat and find a hard bump that seems to move when you swallow. This part of the body is known as the voice box. It is at the upper end of the windpipe. Two vocal cords are stretched across the voice box or larynx in such a way that it leaves a narrow slit between them for the passage of air. | (ii) After listening teacher, students will note it down in their note-books. |
| (iii) Teacher will tell that when the | (iii) Students will note it down in |

| | |
|---|---|
| lungs force air through the slit, the vocal cords vibrate, producing sound. Muscles attached to the vocal cords can make the cords tight or loose. When the vocal cords are tight and thin, the type or quality of voice is different from that when they are loose and thick. | their notebooks. |
| (iv) Teacher will tell that the vocal cords in men are about 20mm long. In women, these are about 5mm shorter. Children have very short vocal cords. This is the reason why the voices of men, women and children are different. | (iv) Students will note it down in their notebooks. |

**(8) Experiment**

| Activity | Discussion | Result |
|---|---|---|
| Take two rubber strips of the same size. Place these two pieces one above the other and stretch them tight. Now blow air through the gap between them. | As the air blows through the stretched rubber strips, a sound is produced. You can also take a piece of paper with a narrow slit and hold it between your fingers. | |
| Now blow through the slit and listen to the sound. | | Our vocal cords produce sound in a similar manner. |

**(9) Recapitulation**

(a) Identify the part that vibrates to produce sound in the following instruments:

(i) Tomtom (ii) Sitar (iii) Flute

(b) Visit the music room of your school. You may also visit musicians in your locality. Make a list of musical instruments. Note down the parts of these instruments that vibrate to produce sound.

**(10) Homework**

(a) If you play a musical instrument, bring it to the class and demonstrate how you play it.

(b) Take a long thread. Place your hands over your ears and get someone to place this thread round your head and hands. Ask her to make the thread tight and hold its ends in one hand. Now ask her to draw her finger and thumb tightly along the thread (Fig. 3.20). Can you hear a rolling sound like that of a thunder? Now repeat the activity while another friend stands near both of you. Can s/he hear any sound?

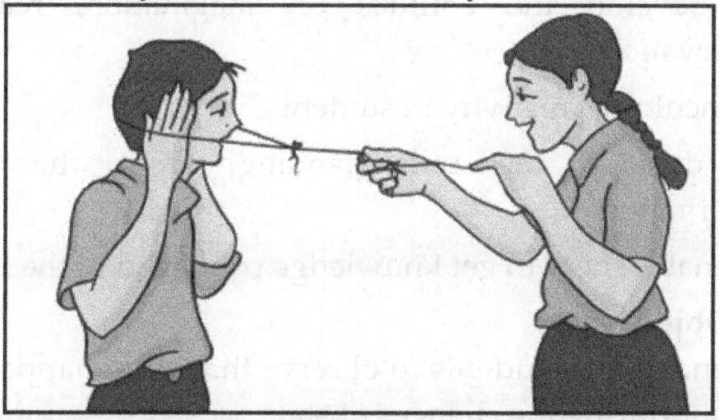

**Fig. 3.20**

> **TECHNOLOGY IS JUST A TOOL. IN TERMS OF GETTING THE KIDS WORKING TOGETHER AND MOTIVATING THEM, THE TEACHER IS THE MOST IMPORTANT**
>
> **— Bill Gates**

# LESSON PLAN – 13

| | |
|---|---|
| **Subject:** Science | **Date:** ________ |
| **Topic:** Can Matter Change its State | **Duration:** 35 – 40 minute |
| | **Class:** 9th |

**(1) General Objectives**

- To develop the interest of students in learning science.
- To develop the abilities of imagination, reasoning and observation.
- To inculcate creativity in students.
- To develop the understanding about the reality and observation.
- To enable them to get knowledge contained in the lesson.

**(2) Specific Objectives**

- To enable the students to observe that what happens inside the matter during the changes of state.
- To enable the students to observe that what happens to the particles of matter during the change of states.
- To enable the students to learn about how this change of state takes place.
- To enable the students to learn about melting point, latent heat, boiling point, etc.
- To enable the students to learn about sublimation of ammonium chloride.

**(3) Previous Knowledge**

The students must have at least general familiarities with matter, its physical nature, characteristics of particles of matter and different states of matter.

**(4) Teaching Aids**

Blackboard, chalk, duster, pointer, camphor or ammonium chloride, china dish, inverted funnel, burner, cotton plug and other useful equipments.

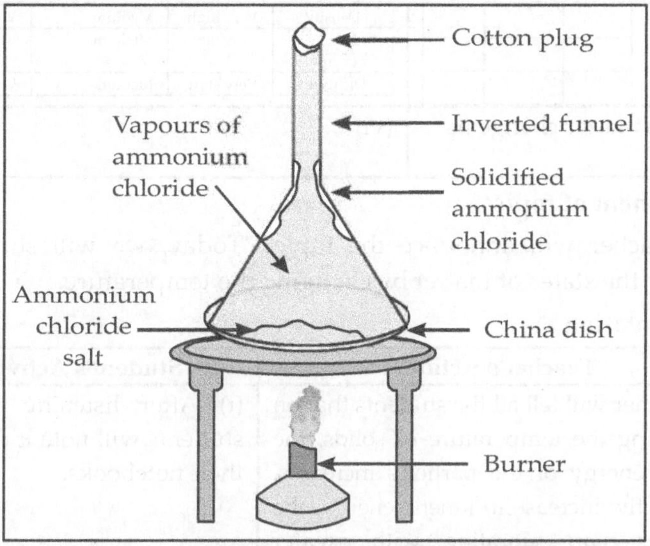


**Fig. 3.21: Sublimation of Ammonium chloride**

## (5) Introduction

<table>
<tr><th>Teacher's Question</th><th>Student's Answer</th></tr>
<tr><td>(i) What do you know about matter in our surroundings?</td><td>(i) Anything that occupies space, possess mass is called Matter.</td></tr>
<tr><td>(ii) Explain about physical nature of matter.</td><td>(ii) Matter is made up of particles. The particles of matter are very small that they are small beyond our imagination.</td></tr>
<tr><td>(iii) What do you know about characteristics of particles of matter?</td><td>(iii) The particles of matter have spaces between them and particles of matter attract each other.</td></tr>
<tr><td>(iv) Very good, now tell me about different states of matter.</td><td>(iv) Matter around us exists in three states. They are:<br>Solids: Ice, stone, sand, gold, iron, etc.<br>Liquids: Water, milk, petrol, cold drink, etc.<br>Gases: Air, oxygen, nitrogen, ammonia, etc.</td></tr>
<tr><td>(v) Fill this table:<br><table><tr><th>Properties</th><th>Solid</th><th>Liquid</th><th>Gas</th></tr><tr><td></td><td></td><td></td><td></td></tr><tr><td></td><td></td><td></td><td></td></tr><tr><td></td><td></td><td></td><td></td></tr><tr><td></td><td></td><td></td><td></td></tr></table></td><td>(v)<br><table><tr><th>Properties</th><th>Solid</th><th>Liquid</th><th>Gas</th></tr><tr><td>Interparticle Spaces</td><td>Very small</td><td>Comparatively large</td><td>Very large</td></tr><tr><td>Interparticle Force</td><td>Very strong</td><td>Weak</td><td>Very weak</td></tr><tr><td>Nature</td><td>Very hard and rigid</td><td>Fluid</td><td>Highly fluid</td></tr><tr><td>Compressibility</td><td>Negligible</td><td>Very small</td><td>Highly compressible</td></tr></table></td></tr>
</table>

| | | | | | | | |
|---|---|---|---|---|---|---|---|
| | | | | Density | Very high | Medium | Very low |
| | | | | Kinetic energy | Very low | Medium | Very high |
| | | | | Diffusion | Very slow | Medium | Very high |
| (vi) Can matter change its state? | | | | (vi) .................... | | | |

**(6) Statement of topic**

Now, teacher will announce the topic, "Today, we will study about changing the states of matter by changing the temperature."

**(7) Presentation**

| Teacher's Action | Student's Activity |
|---|---|
| (i) Teacher will tell all the students that on increasing the temperature of solids, the kinetic energy of the particles increases. Due to the increase in kinetic energy, the particles start vibrating with greater speed. The energy supplied by heat overcomes the forces of attraction between the particles. The particles leave their fixed positions and start moving more freely. A stage is reached when the solid melts and is converted to a liquid. The temperature at which a solid melts to become a liquid at the atmospheric pressure is called its melting point. | (i) After listening teacher, students will note it down in their notebooks. |
| (ii) Teacher will tell that the melting point of ice is 273.16 K. The process of melting, that is, change of solid state into liquid state is also known as fusion. | (ii) Students will note it down in their notebooks. Some students ask that when a solid melts, its temperature remains the same, so where does the heat energy go? |
| (iii) Teacher will tell that you must have observed, during the experiment of melting, that the temperature of the system does not change after the melting point is reached, till all the ice melts. This happens even though we continue to heat the beaker, that is, we continue to supply heat. This heat gets used up in changing the state by overcoming the forces of | (iii) Students will note it down in their notebooks. |

| | |
|---|---|
| attraction between the particles. As this heat energy is absorbed by ice without showing any rise in temperature, it is considered that it gets hidden into the contents of the beaker and is known as the latent heat. The word latent means hidden. The amount of heat energy that is required to change 1 kg of a solid into liquid at atmospheric pressure at its melting point is known as the latent heat of fusion. So, particles in water at 0°C (273 K) have more energy as compared to particles in ice at the same temperature. | |
| (iv) Teacher will tell that when we supply heat energy to water, particles start moving even faster. At a certain temperature, a point is reached when the particles have enough energy to break free from the forces of attraction of each other. At this temperature, the liquid starts changing into gas. The temperature at which a liquid starts boiling at the atmospheric pressure is known as its boiling point. Boiling is a bulk phenomenon. Particles from the bulk of the liquid gain enough energy to change into the vapour state. | (iv) Students will note it down in their notebooks. |
| (v) Teacher will tell that therefore, we infer that the state of matter can be changed into another state by changing the temperature. | (v) Students will note it down in their notebooks. |

**(8) Experiment**

| Activity | Discussion | Result |
|---|---|---|
| Take a pinch of camphor or ammonium chloride. Crush it and put it in a china dish. Put an inverted funnel over the china dish. Put a cotton plug on the | What do you infer from this activity? | On heating, ammonium chloride changes into white vapours. These vapours rise up and get converted into solid ammonium chloride on coming in |

| | | |
|---|---|---|
| stem of the funnel. Now, heat slowly and observe. | | contact with the cold, inner walls of the funnel. In this way, ammonium chloride collects on the inner sides of the funnel in the form of a sublimate and can be removed. |

**(9) Recapitulation**

- What happens inside the matter during the change of state?
- What happens to the particles of matter during the change of states?
- How does this change of state take place?
- For any substance, why does the temperature remain constant during the change of state?

**(10) Homework**

- Suggest a method to liquefy atmospheric gases.
- What produces more severe burns, boiling water or steam?

> **EXPERIENCE IS A HARD TEACHER BECAUSE SHE GIVES THE TEST FIRST, THE LESSON AFTERWARD.**
>
> **— Vernon Law**

# LESSON PLAN – 14

| **Subject:** Science | **Date:** ________ |
|---|---|
| **Topic:** Atom | **Duration:** 35 – 40 minute |
| | **Class:** 9th |

**(1) General Objectives**

- To develop the interest of students in learning science.
- To develop the abilities of imagination, reasoning and observation.
- To inculcate creativity in students.
- To develop the understanding about the reality and observation.
- To enable them to get knowledge contained in the lesson.

**(2) Specific Objectives**

- To enable the students to learn about atoms.
- To enable the students to know about symbols of atoms of different elements.
- To enable the students to know about IUPAC.
- To enable the students to learn about Atomic Mass, Atomic Mass Unit (AMU), etc.
- To enable the students to learn about how do atoms exist.

**(3) Previous Knowledge**

The students must have at least general familiarities with matter (substance), mass, element, compound, mixture, laws of chemical combination, i.e. law of conservation of mass, law of constant proportions, etc.

**(4) Teaching Aids**

Blackboard, chalk, duster, pointer and other useful equipments.

**Table 3.5: Symbols for some elements**

| Element | Symbol | Element | Symbol | Element | Symbol |
|---|---|---|---|---|---|
| Aluminium | Al | Copper | Cu | Nitrogen | N |
| Argon | Ar | Flourine | F | Oxygen | O |
| Barium | Ba | Gold | Au | Potassium | K |

| Boron | B | Hydrogen | H | Silicon | Si |
|---|---|---|---|---|---|
| Bromine | Br | Iodine | I | Silver | Ag |
| Calcium | Ca | Iron | Fe | Sodium | Na |
| Carbon | C | Lead | Pb | Sulphur | S |
| Chlorine | Cl | Magnesium | Mg | Uranium | U |
| Cobalt | Co | Neon | Ne | Zinc | Zn |

**Table 3.6 Atomic Masses of a few elements**

| Element | Atomic Mass |
|---|---|
| Hydrogen | 1 |
| Carbon | 12 |
| Nitrogen | 14 |
| Oxygen | 16 |
| Sodium | 23 |
| Magnesium | 24 |
| Sulphur | 32 |
| Chlorine | 35.5 |
| Calcium | 40 |

### (5) Introduction

| Teacher's Question | Student's Answer |
|---|---|
| (i) What do you know about matter (substance)? | (i) Anything that occupies space, possess mass is called matter (substance). |
| (ii) What do you know about mass, element, compound, mixture? | (ii) Mass is a dimensionless quantity representing the amount of matter in a particle or an object. An element is a fundamental, essential or irreducible constituent of a composite entity. Compound is a combination of two or more elements or parts. A mixture is a material system made up of two or more different substances that are mixed but are not combined chemically. |
| (iii) Good, do you know about laws of chemical combination? | (iii) Yes, law of conservation of mass and law of constant proportion. |
| (iii) Very good, now tell me about Dalton's atomic theory. | (iii) ................................ |
| (iv) What is an atom? | (iv)............................... |

**(6) Statement of topic**

Now, teacher will announce the topic, "Today, we will study about atom."

**(7) Presentation**

| Teacher's Action | Student's Activity |
|---|---|
| (i) Teacher will tell all the students that an atom is the smallest particle of the element that can exist independently and retain all its chemical properties. | (i) After listening teacher, students will note it down in their notebooks. |
| (ii) Teacher will tell that atoms are very small; they are smaller than anything that we can imagine or compare with. More than millions of atoms when stacked would make a layer barely as thick as this sheet of paper. | (ii) Students will note it down in their notebooks. |
| (iii) Teacher will tell that Dalton was the first scientist to use the symbols for elements in a very specific sense. When he used a symbol for an element, he also meant a definite quantity of that element, that is, one atom of that element. Berzilius suggested that the symbols of elements could be made from one or two letters of the name of the element. In the beginning, the names of elements were derived from the name of the place where they were found for the first time. For example, the name copper was taken from Cyprus. Some names were taken from specific colours. For example, gold was taken from the English word meaning yellow. Nowadays, IUPAC (International Union of Pure and Applied Chemistry) approves names of | (iii) Students will note it down in their notebooks. Some students ask about some symbols. |

| | |
|---|---|
| elements. Many of the symbols are the first one or two letters of the element's name in English. The first letter of a symbol is always written as a capital letter (uppercase) and the second letter as a small letter (lowercase).<br>For example: (i) hydrogen, H, (ii) aluminium, Al and not AL and (iii) cobalt, Co and not CO.<br>Symbols of some elements are formed from the first letter of the name and a letter, appearing later in the name. Examples are: (i) chlorine, Cl, (ii) zinc, Zn, etc.<br>Other symbols have been taken from the names of elements in Latin, German or Greek. For example, the symbol of iron is Fe from its Latin name Ferrum, sodium is Na from Natrium and potassium is K from Kalium. Therefore, each element has a name and a unique chemical symbol. | |
| (iv) Teacher will tell that table 3.5 is given for you to refer to whenever you study about elements. Do not bother to memorise all in one go. With the passage of time and repeated usage, you will automatically be able to reproduce the symbols. | (iv) Students will draw the table into their notebooks. |
| (v) Now, the teacher will tell that the most remarkable concept that Dalton's atomic theory proposed was that of the atomic mass. According to him, each element had a characteristic atomic mass. | (v) Students will note it down in their notebooks.<br>Some students ask about atomic mass. |
| (vi)Teacher will tell that carbon-12 | (vi) Students will note it down in |

| | |
|---|---|
| isotope was chosen as the standard reference for measuring atomic masses. One atomic mass unit is a mass unit equal to exactly one twelfth (1/12th) the mass of one atom of carbon-12. The relative atomic masses of all elements have been found with respect to an atom of carbon-12. | their notebooks.<br>Some students ask about atomic masses of a few elements. |
| (vii) Teacher will tell that table 3.6 is given for you to refer to atomic masses of a few elements. | (vii) Students will draw the table in their notebooks.<br>Some students ask that how do atoms exist. |
| (viii) Teacher will tell that atoms of most elements are not able to exist independently. Atoms form molecules and ions. These molecules or ions aggregate in large numbers to form the matter that we can see, feel or touch. | (viii) Students will note it down in their notebooks. |

**(8) Experiment**

| Activity | Discussion | Result |
|---|---|---|
| Imagine a fruit seller selling fruits without any standard weight with him. He takes a watermelon and says, "this has a mass equal to 12 units" (12 watermelon units or 12 fruit mass units). He makes twelve equal pieces of the watermelon and finds the mass of each fruit he is selling, relative to the mass of one piece of the watermelon. Now he sells his fruits by relative fruit mass unit (fmu). | Here, the fruit mass unit is as same as atomic mass unit. | Thus, the relative atomic mass of the atom of an element is defined as the average mass of the atom, as compared to 1/12th the mass of one carbon-12 atom. |

**(9) Recapitulation**

- Define the atomic mass unit.
- Name the first scientist who uses the symbols for elements.

**(10) Homework**

- Define an atom in your own words.
- Write symbols for the following elements:

  (a) Zinc

  (b) Chlorine

  (c) Aluminium

> **PROSPERITY IS A GREAT TEACHER; ADVERSITY A GREATER.**
>
> **— William Hazlitt**

# LESSON PLAN – 15

| | |
|---|---|
| **Subject:** Science | **Date:** ________ |
| **Topic:** Organisation of a cell | **Duration:** 35 – 40 minutes |
| | **Class:** 9th |

**(1) General Objectives**

- To develop the interest of students in learning science.
- To develop the abilities of imagination, reasoning and observation.
- To inculcate creativity in students.
- To develop the understanding about the reality and observation.
- To enable them to get knowledge contained in the lesson.

**(2) Specific Objectives**

- To enable the students to learn how a cell is organised.
- To enable the students to know about plasma membrane, nucleus and cytoplasm.
- To enable the students to learn about osmosis.
- To enable the students to learn about what will happen if we put an animal cell or a plant cell into a solution of sugar or salt in water.
- To enable the students to do an activity, i.e. osmosis with an egg.

**(3) Previous Knowledge**

The students must have at least general familiarities with cells, its founder, structure, functions, etc.

**(4) Teaching Aids**

Blackboard, chalk, duster, pointer, egg, dilute hydrochloric acid, pure water, concentrated salt solution and other required material, etc.

**(5) Introduction**

| Teacher's Question | Student's Answer |
|---|---|
| (i) What do you know about cell? | (i) It is the structural and functional unit of life. |

| | |
|---|---|
| (ii) Who discovered cells? | (ii) Robert Hooke discovered the cells in 1665. |
| (iii) Good, what is the function of a cell? | (iii) A cell is able to live and perform all its functions because of various organelles. |
| (iv) What do you know about organelles? | (iv) A specialised cellular part (as a mitochondrion, lysosome or ribosome) that is analogous to an organ. |
| (v) What is a cell made up of? | (v) ........................ |
| (vi) What is the structural organisation of a cell? | (vi)........................ |

**(6) Statement of topic**

Now, teacher will announce the topic, "Today, we will study about structural organisation of a cell."

**(7) Presentation**

| Teacher's Action | Student's Activity |
|---|---|
| (i) Teacher will tell all the students that if we study a cell under a microscope, we would come across three features in almost every cell, i.e. plasma membrane, nucleus and cytoplasm. All activities inside the cell and interactions of the cell with its environment are possible due to these features. | (i) After listening teacher, students will note it down in their notebooks. |
| (ii) Teacher will tell that plasma membrane or cell membrane is the outermost covering of the cell that separates the contents of the cell from its external environment. The plasma membrane allows or permits the entry and exit of some materials in and out of the cell. It also prevents movement of some other materials. The cell membrane, therefore, is called a selectively permeable membrane. | (ii) Students will note it down in their notebooks. |
| (iii) Teacher will tell that the movement of water molecules through such a selectively | (iii) Students will note it down in their notebooks. Some students ask that what will |

| | |
|---|---|
| permeable membrane is called osmosis. The movement of water across the plasma membrane is also affected by the amount of substance dissolved in water.<br>Thus, osmosis is the passage of water from a region of high water concentration through a semi-permeable membrane to a region of low water concentration. | happen if we put an animal cell or a plant cell into a solution of sugar or salt in water. |
| (iv) Teacher will tell that one of the following three things could happen:<br>(a) If the medium surrounding the cell has a higher water concentration than the cell, meaning that the outside solution is very dilute, the cell will gain water by osmosis. Such a solution is known as a hypotonic solution. Water molecules are free to pass across the cell membrane in both directions, but more water will come into the cell than will leave. The net (overall) result is that water enters the cell. The cell is likely to swell up.<br>(b) If the medium has exactly the same water concentration as the cell, there will be no net movement of water across the cell membrane. Such a solution is known as an isotonic solution. Water crosses the cell membrane in both directions, but the amount going in is the same as the amount going out, so there is no overall movement of water. The cell will stay in the same size as before.<br>(c) If the medium has a lower concentration of water than the cell, | (iv) Students will note it down in their notebooks. |

| | |
|---|---|
| meaning that it is a very concentrated solution, the cell will lose water by osmosis. Such a solution is known as a hypertonic solution. Again, water crosses the cell membrane in both directions, but this time more water leaves the cell than enters it. Therefore the cell will shrink. Thus, osmosis is a special case of diffusion through a selectively permeable membrane. | |
| (v) Teacher will tell that the nucleus is a membrane bound structure that contains the cell's hereditary information and controls the cell's growth and reproduction. It is commonly the most prominent organelle in the cell. | (v) Students will note it down in their notebooks. |
| (vi) Teacher will tell that the cytoplasm consists of all of the contents outside the nucleus and enclosed within the cell membrane of a cell. This includes the cytosol and in euckaryotic cells, organelles such as mitochondria and ribosomes. Also located within the cytoplasm is the cytoskeleton, a network of fibres that help the cell maintain its shape and give it support. | (vi) Students will note it down in their notebooks. |

**(8) Experiment**

| Activity | Discussion | Result |
|---|---|---|
| Remove the shell of an egg by dissolving it in dilute hydrochloric acid. The shell is mostly calcium carbonate. A thin outer skin now encloses the egg. Put the egg in pure water and | What do we observe? | The egg swells because water passes into it by osmosis. |

| | | |
|---|---|---|
| observe after 5 minutes. | | |
| Place a similar de-shelled egg in a concentrated salt solution and observe for 5 minutes. | | The egg shrinks. Water passes out of the egg solution into the salt solution because the salt solution is more concentrated. |

**(9) Recapitulation**

- Make a comparison and write down ways in which plant cells are different from animal cells.
- How is a prokaryotic cell different from a eukaryotic cell?

**(10) Homework**

- How does an Amoeba obtain its food?
- What is osmosis?

WHEN YOU STUDY GREAT TEACHERS...YOU WILL LEARN MUCH MORE FROM THEIR CARING AND HARD WORK THAN FROM THEIR STYLE.

— **William Glasser**

# LESSON PLAN – 16

| | |
|---|---|
| **Subject:** Science | **Date:** ________ |
| **Topic:** Acceleration | **Duration:** 35 – 40 minutes |
| | **Class:** 9th |

**(1) General Objectives**

- To develop the interest of students in learning science.
- To develop the abilities of imagination, reasoning and observation.
- To inculcate creativity in students.
- To develop the understanding about the reality and observation.
- To enable them to get knowledge contained in the lesson.

**(2) Specific Objectives**

- To enable the students to learn about how to express the change in velocity of an object.
- To enable the students to know about acceleration.
- To enable the students to know about uniform and non-uniform acceleration.
- To enable the students to calculate the acceleration.

**(3) Previous Knowledge**

The students must have at least general familiarities with motions, motion along a straight line, distance, displacement, uniform motion and non-uniform motion, speed, velocity, average speed, average velocity, etc.

**(4) Teaching Aids**

Blackboard, chalk, duster, pointer, models and other required materials.

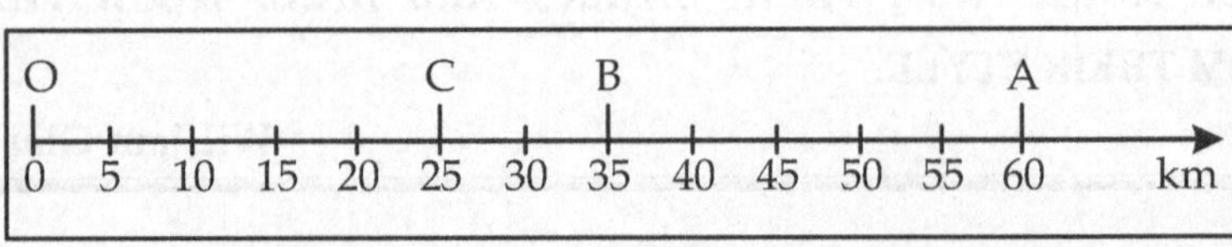


**Fig. 3.22: Positions of an object on a straight-line path**

**(5) Introduction**

| Teacher's Question | Student's Answer |
|---|---|
| (i) What do you know about motion? | (i) When the position of an object changes with time is known as motion. |
| (ii) Good, tell me about a motion along a straight line. | (ii) The simplest type of motion is the motion along a straight line. It is the motion of an object moving along a straight path. |
| (iii) Well, now tell me about distance and displacement. | (iii) Distance is the amount of separation between two objects or two points.<br>The shortest distance measured from the initial to the final position of an object is known as the displacement. |
| (iv) Very good, now tell me that do you have any idea about uniform and non-uniform motion. | (iv) Yes, when a body covers equal distance in equal intervals of time then the body is said to be in a uniform motion.<br>When a body moves unequal distances in equal intervals of time or vice-versa, then the body is said to be in non-uniform motion. |
| (v) Explain speed, velocity, average speed and average velocity. | (v) Speed is distance covered per unit time.<br>Velocity is the rate of change of the position of an object, equivalent to a specification of its speed and direction of motion.<br>The average speed of an object is the motion along a straight line at a variable speed.<br>The average velocity of an object is when we express magnitude of the average speed of the object in motion. |
| (vi) Good, now tell me about rate of change of velocity, i.e. acceleration. | (vi)...................... |

**(6) Statement of topic**

Now, teacher will announce the topic, "Today, we will study about acceleration."

**(7) Presentation**

| Teacher's Action | Student's Activity |
|---|---|
| (i) Teacher will tell all the students that during uniform motion of an object along a straight line, the velocity remains constant with time. In this case, the change in velocity of the object for any time interval is zero. However, in non-uniform motion, velocity varies with time. It has different values at different instants and at different points of the path. Thus, the change in velocity of the object during any time interval is not zero. | (i) After listening teacher, students will note it down in their notebooks. Some students ask that can we now express the change in velocity of an object. |
| (ii) Teacher will tell that to answer such a question, we have to introduce another physical quantity called acceleration, which is a measure of the change in the velocity of an object per unit time. That is, $\text{acceleration} = \dfrac{\text{change in velocity}}{\text{time taken}}$ If the velocity of an object changes from an initial value u to the final value v in time t, the acceleration a is, $a = \dfrac{v-u}{t}$ This kind of motion is known as accelerated motion. The acceleration is taken to be positive if it is in the direction of velocity and negative when it is opposite to the direction of velocity. The SI unit of acceleration is m $s^{-2}$. | (ii) Students will note it down in their notebooks. Some students ask about uniform and non-uniform acceleration. |
| (iii) Teacher will tell that if an object travels in a straight line and its velocity increases or decreases by equal amounts in equal | (iii) Students will note it down in their notebooks. |

| | |
|---|---|
| intervals of time, then the acceleration of the object is said to be uniform. The motion of a freely falling body is an example of uniformly accelerated motion. On the other hand, an object can travel with non-uniform acceleration if its velocity changes at a non-uniform rate. For example, if a car travelling along a straight road increases its speed by unequal amounts in equal intervals of time, then the car is said to be moving with non-uniform acceleration. | |

**(8) Sample Problem**

| Problem | Solution |
|---|---|
| Starting from a stationary position, Mehul paddles his bicycle to attain a velocity of 6m $s^{-1}$ in 30 s. Then he applies brakes such that the velocity of the bicycle comes down to 4 m $s^{-1}$ in the next 5s. Calculate the acceleration of the bicycle in both the cases. | In the first case: initial velocity, $u$ = 0 m $s^{-1}$; final velocity, $v$ = 6m $s^{-1}$; time, $t$ = 30s.<br>we have $a = \frac{v-u}{t}$<br>Substituting the given values of $u$, $v$ and $t$ in the above equation, we get<br>$a = \frac{(6\text{ms}^{-1} - 0\text{ms}^{-1})}{30\text{s}} = 0.2\text{ms}^{-2}$<br>In the second case: initial velocity, u = 6 $ms^{-1}$; final velocity, v = 4 $ms^{-1}$; time, t = 5s.<br>Then, $a = \frac{(4\text{ms}^{-1} - 6\text{ms}^{-1})}{5\text{s}} = -0.4\text{ms}^{-2}$<br>The acceleration of the bicycle in the first case is 0.2 $ms^{-2}$ and in the second case, it is –0.4 $ms^{-2}$. |

**(9) Recapitulation**

- When will you say a body is in (a) uniform acceleration (b) non-uniform acceleration?
- A bus decreases its speed from 80 km $h^{-1}$ to 60 km $h^{-1}$ in 5 second. Find the acceleration of the bus.

- A train starting from a railway station and moving with uniform acceleration attains a speed 40 km $h^{-1}$ in 10 minutes. Find its acceleration.

**(10) Homework**

- An athlete completes one round of a circular track of diameter 200 m in 40 s. What will be the distance covered and the displacement at the end of 2 minutes 20 s?
- Joseph jogs from one end A to the other end B of a straight 300 m road in 2 minutes 50 seconds, then turns around and jogs 100 m back to point C in another 1 minute. What are Joseph's average speeds and velocities in jogging (a) from A to B and (b) from A to C?
- Abdul, while driving to school, computes the average speed for his trip to be 20 km $h^{-1}$. On his return trip along the same route, there is less traffic and the average speed is 40 km $h^{-1}$. What is the average speed for Abdul's trip?
- A motorboat starting from rest on a lake accelerates in a straight line at a constant rate of 3.0 m $s^{-2}$ for 8.0 s. How far does the boat travel during this time?

# LESSON PLAN – 17

| **Subject:** Science | **Date:** ________ |
|---|---|
| **Topic:** Second law of motion | **Duration:** 35 – 40 minutes |
| | **Class:** 9th |

## (1) General Objectives

- To develop the interest of students in learning science.
- To develop the abilities of imagination, reasoning and observation.
- To inculcate creativity in students.
- To develop the understanding about the reality and observation.
- To enable them to get knowledge contained in the lesson.

## (2) Specific Objectives

- To enable the students to know, how the acceleration of an object depends on the force applied to it and how we measure a force.
- To enable the students to learn about momentum.
- To enable the students to know about second law of motion.
- To enable the students to derive mathematical formulation of second law of motion.
- To enable the students to derive first law of motion using second law of motion.

## (3) Previous Knowledge

The students must have at least general familiarities with mass, velocity, acceleration, force, state of motion, first law of motion, inertia and mass.

## (4) Teaching Aids

Blackboard, chalk, duster, pointer, models and other required materials.

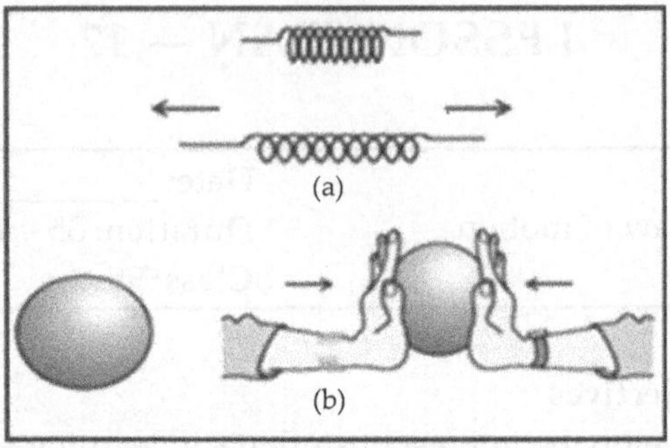


**Fig. 3.23: (a) A spring expands on application of force; (b) A spherical rubber ball becomes oblong as we apply force on it.**

## (5) Introduction

| Teacher's Question | Student's Answer |
|---|---|
| (i) What do you know about mass? | (i) Mass is a dimensionless quantity representing the amount of matter in a particle or object. |
| (ii) What do you know about velocity? | (ii) Velocity is the rate of change of the position of an object, equivalent to a specification of its speed and direction of motion. |
| (iii) Good, now tell me about acceleration. | (iii) Acceleration is a measure of the change in the velocity of an object per unit time. |
| (iv) Well, do you have any idea about force? | (iv) It is a push or a pull on an object. |
| (v) When does a force come into play? | (v) When the interaction between two objects arises. |
| (vi) Moving a book placed on a table is which kind of action pushing, pulling, lifting or all of these? | (vi) Push and pull. |
| (vii) Tell me about some uses of forces. | (vii) A force can be used to change the magnitude of velocity of an object or to change its direction of motion. We also know that a force can change the shape and size of some objects. |
| (viii) Good, what do you know about state of motion? | (viii) It is described by its speed and the direction of motion. |
| (ix) Do you know about first law | (ix) Yes, it is stated as an object |

| | |
|---|---|
| of motion? | remains in a state of rest or of uniform motion in a straight line unless compelled to change that state by an applied force. |
| (x) Well now then tell me about inertia and give the reason that why the first law of motion is known as law of inertia. | (x) All objects resist a change in their state of motion. In a qualitative way, the tendency of undisturbed objects to stay at rest or to keep moving with the same velocity is called inertia. This is why, the first law of motion is also known as the law of inertia. |
| (xi) Do all bodies have the same inertia? | (xi) No, different bodies have different inertia according to their masses. |
| (xii) Well done, now do you know about second law of motion? | (xii) ................................ |

**(6) Statement of topic**

Now, teacher will announce the topic, "Today, we will study the Second law of motion."

**(7) Presentation**

| Teacher's Action | Student's Activity |
|---|---|
| (i) Teacher will tell all the students that the first law of motion indicates that when an unbalanced external force acts on an object, its velocity changes, that is, the object gets an acceleration. We would now like to study how the acceleration of an object depends on the force applied to it and how we measure a force. Let us recount some observations from our everyday life. During the game of table tennis, if the ball hits a player it does not hurt him. On the other hand, when a fast moving cricket ball hits a spectator, it may hurt him. A truck at rest does not require any attention when parked along a roadside. But a moving truck, even at | (i) After listening teacher, students will note it down in their notebooks. |

| | |
|---|---|
| speeds as low as 5 m $s^{-1}$, may kill a person standing in its path. A small mass, such as a bullet may kill a person when fired from a gun. These observations suggest that the impact produced by the objects depends on their mass and velocity. Similarly, if an object is to be accelerated, we know that a greater force is required to give a greater velocity. In other words, there appears to exist some quantity of importance that combines the object's mass and its velocity. One such property called momentum was introduced by Newton. The momentum, p of an object is defined as the product of its mass, m and velocity, v. That is, p = mv. Momentum has both direction and magnitude. Its direction is the same as that of velocity, v. The SI unit of momentum is kilogram-metre per second (kg m $s^{-1}$). Since the application of an unbalanced force brings a change in the velocity of the object, it is therefore clear that a force also produces a change of momentum. | |
| (ii) Teacher will tell that let us consider a situation in which a car with a dead battery is to be pushed along a straight road to give it a speed of 1 m $s^{-1}$, which is sufficient to start its engine. If one or two persons give a sudden push (unbalanced force) to it, it hardly starts. But a continuous push over some time results in a gradual acceleration of the car to this speed. It means that the change of momentum of the car is not only determined by the magnitude of the force but also by the time during which the force is exerted. It may then also be concluded that the force | (ii) Students will note it down in their notebooks. |

| | |
|---|---|
| necessary to change the momentum of an object depends on the time rate at which the momentum is changed.<br>The second law of motion states that the rate of change of momentum of an object is proportional to the applied unbalanced force in the direction of force. | |
| (iii) Teacher will tell that the second law of motion states that the rate of change of momentum of an object is proportional to the applied unbalanced force in the direction of force. | (iii) Students will note it down in their notebooks.<br>Some students ask for mathematical formulation of second law of motion. |
| (iv) Teacher will tell that suppose an object of mass, m is moving along a straight line with an initial velocity, u. It is uniformly accelerated to velocity, v in time, t by the application of a constant force, F throughout the time, t.<br>The initial and final momentum of the object will be, $p_1$ = mu and $p_2$ = mv respectively.<br>Here, [a = (v – u)/t] is the acceleration, which is the rate of change of velocity.<br>The quantity, k is a constant of proportionality. The SI units of mass and acceleration are kg and m $s^{-2}$ respectively. The unit of force is so chosen that the value of the constant, k becomes one. For this, one unit of force is defined as the amount that produces an acceleration of 1 m $s^{-2}$ in an object of 1 kg mass. That is, 1 unit of force = k × (1 kg) × (1 m $s^{-2}$).<br>Thus, the value of k becomes 1.<br>F = ma (a)<br>The unit of force is kg m $s^{-2}$ or Newton, which has the symbol N. The second law of motion gives us a method to measure the force acting on an object as | (iv) Students will note it down in their notebooks.<br>Some students ask that can we state first law of motion with the help of second law of motion. |

| | |
|---|---|
| a product of its mass and acceleration. | |
| (v) Teacher will tell that the first law of motion can be mathematically stated from the mathematical expression of the second law of motion. Eq. (a) is $F = ma$ or $F = \frac{m(v-u)}{t}$ (b) or $Ft = mv - mu$ That is, when F = 0, v = u for whatever time, t is taken. This means that the object will continue moving with uniform velocity, u throughout the time, t. If u is zero then v will also be zero. That is, the object will remain at rest. | (v) Students will note it down in their notebooks. |

**(8) Sample problems**

| Problems | Solutions |
|---|---|
| (i) A motorcar is moving with a velocity of 108 km/h and it takes 4 s to stop after the brakes are applied. Calculate the force exerted by the brakes on the motorcar if its mass along with the passengers is 1000 kg. | (i) The initial velocity of the motorcar u = 108 km/h = 108 × 1000 m/(60 × 60 s) = 30 m $s^{-1}$ and the final velocity of the motorcar v = 0 m $s^{-1}$. The total mass of the motorcar along with its passengers = 1000 kg and the time taken to stop the motorcar, t = 4s. From Eq. (b) we have the magnitude of the force applied by the brakes F as m(v – u)/t. On substituting the values, we get F = 1000 kg × (0 – 30) m $s^{-1}$/4 s = – 7500 kg m $s^{-2}$ or – 7500 N. The negative sign tells us that the force exerted by the brakes is opposite to the direction of motion of the motorcar. |
| (ii) A force of 5 N gives a mass $m_1$, an acceleration of 10 m $s^{-2}$ and a mass $m_2$, an acceleration of 20 m $s^{-2}$. What acceleration would it give if both the masses were tied together? | (ii) From Eq. (a) we have $m_1 = F/a_1$ and $m_2 = F/a_2$. Here, $a_1$ = 10 m $s^{-2}$; $a_2$ = 20 m $s^{-2}$ and F = 5 N. Thus, $m_1$ = 5 N/10 m $s^{-2}$ = 0.50 kg; and $m_2$ = 5 N/20 m $s^{-2}$ = 0.25 kg. If the two masses were tied together, the total mass, m would be m = 0.50 kg + 0.25 kg = 0.75 kg. |

| | The acceleration, a produced in the combined mass by the 5 N force would be, a = F/m = 5 N/0.75 kg = 6.67 m $s^{-2}$. |
|---|---|

**(9) Recapitulation**

- An object experiences a net zero external unbalanced force. Is it possible for the object to be travelling with a non-zero velocity? If yes, state the conditions that must be placed on the magnitude and direction of the velocity. If no, provide a reason.
- When a carpet is beaten with a stick, dust comes out of it. Give reason.
- Why is it advised to tie any luggage kept on the roof of a bus with a rope?

**(10) Homework**

- An automobile vehicle has a mass of 1500 kg. What must be the force between the vehicle and road if the vehicle is to be stopped with a negative acceleration of 1.7 m $s^{-2}$?
- What is the momentum of an object of mass m, moving with a velocity v?

  (a) $(mv)^2$ (b) $mv^2$ (c) ½ $mv^2$ (d) mv

**COME FORTH INTO THE LIGHT OF THINGS, LET NATURE BE YOUR TEACHER.**

**— William Wordsworth**

# LESSON PLAN – 18

| **Subject:** Science | **Date:** _______ |
|---|---|
| **Topic:** Weight of an object on the moon | **Duration:** 35 – 40 minutes |
| | **Class:** 9th |

**(1) General Objectives**

- To develop the interest of students in learning science.
- To develop the abilities of imagination, reasoning and observation.
- To inculcate creativity in students.
- To develop the understanding about the reality and observation.
- To enable them to get knowledge contained in the lesson.

**(2) Specific Objectives**

- To enable the students to learn about mass of an object.
- To enable the students to learn about weight of an object.
- To enable the students to learn about differences between the mass of an object and its weight on the moon.
- To enable the students to observe that why is the weight of an object on the moon $1/6^{th}$ its weight on the earth.

**(3) Previous Knowledge**

The students must have at least general familiarities with centripetal force, gravitation, universal law of gravitation, importance of the universal law of gravitation, free fall, acceleration due to gravity, value of g, etc.

**(4) Teaching Aids**

Blackboard, chalk, duster, pointer, models and other required materials, etc.

**Table 3.7**

| Celestial body | Mass (kg) | Radius (m) |
|---|---|---|
| Earth | $5.98 \times 10^{24}$ | $6.37 \times 10^{6}$ |
| Moon | $7.36 \times 10^{22}$ | $1.74 \times 10^{6}$ |

## (5) Introduction

| Teacher's Question | Student's Answer |
|---|---|
| (i) What do you know about centripetal force? | (i) It makes a body to follow a curved path. |
| (ii) What do you know about gravitation? | (ii) It is a force of attraction exerted by each particle of matter in the universe on every other particle. |
| (iii) Good, define universal law of gravitation. | (iii) According to the universal law of gravitation, the force between two objects is directly proportional to the product of their masses. |
| (iv) Good, tell me about the importance of the universal law of gravitation. | (iv) The universal law of gravitation successfully explained several phenomena which were believed to be unconnected:<br>(a) the force that binds us to the earth;<br>(b) the motion of the moon around the earth;<br>(c) the motion of planets around the Sun; and<br>(d) the tides due to the moon and the Sun. |
| (v) Well, now tell me about free fall. | (v) Whenever objects fall towards the earth under gravitational force alone, we say that the objects are in free fall. |
| (vi) Is there any change in the velocity of falling objects? | (vi) Yes, due to gravitation, there is change in the velocity of falling objects. |
| (vii) Calculate the value of g. | (vii) To calculate the value of g, we should put the values of G, M and R in Eq. $g = G\frac{M}{d^2}$ namely, universal gravitational constant, G = $6.7 \times 10^{-11}$ N $m^2$ $kg^{-2}$, mass of the earth, M = $6 \times 10^{24}$ kg, and radius of the earth, R = $6.4 \times 10^6$ m.<br>$g = G\frac{M}{R^2}$<br>$= \frac{6.7 \times 10^{-11} Nm^2kg^{-2} \times 6 \times 10^{24} kg}{(6.4 \times 10^6 m)^2} = 9.8 ms^{-2}$<br>Thus, the value of acceleration due to gravity of the earth, g = 9.8 m $s^{-2}$. |
| (vii) What do you know about mass of an object? | (vii) .......................... |
| (viii) What do you know about weight of an object? | (viii).......................... |

**(6) Statement of topic**

Now, teacher will announce the topic, "Today, we will study about weight of an object on the moon."

**(7) Presentation**

| Teacher's Action | Student's Activity |
|---|---|
| (i) Teacher will tell all the students that the mass of an object is a fundamental property of the object, a numerical measure of its inertia, a fundamental measure of the amount of matter in the object. | (i) After listening teacher, students will note it down in their notebooks. Some students ask about weight. |
| (ii) Teacher will discuss that the earth attracts every object with a certain force and now tells that this force depends on the mass (m) of the object and the acceleration due to the gravity (g). The weight of an object is the force with which it is attracted towards the earth. We know that<br>$F = m \times a$, ...(a)<br>that is,<br>$F = m \times g$ ...(b)<br>The force of attraction of the earth on an object is known as the weight of the object. It is denoted by W. Substituting the same in Eq. (b), we have<br>$W = m \times g$ ...(c)<br>As the weight of an object is the force with which it is attracted towards the earth, the SI unit of weight is the same as that of force, that is, newton (N). The weight is a force acting vertically downwards; it has both magnitude and direction. | (ii) Students will note it down in their notebooks.<br>Some students ask about the differences between the mass of an object and its weight. |
| (iii) Teacher will tell that mass is a measure of how much matter an object has. Weight is a measure of how strongly gravity pulls on that matter. Thus, if you were to travel to the moon your weight would change because the pull of gravity is weaker | (iii) Students will note it down in their notebooks. |

| | |
|---|---|
| there than on Earth but, your mass would stay the same because you are still made up of the same amount of matter. | |
| (iv) Teacher will tell that we have learnt about the weight of an object on the earth is the force with which the earth attracts the object. In the same way, the weight of an object on the moon is the force with which the moon attracts that object. The mass of the moon is less than that of the earth. Due to this, the moon exerts lesser force of attraction on objects. Let the mass of an object be m. Let its weight on the moon be $W_m$. Let the mass of the moon be $M_m$ and its radius be $R_m$. By applying the universal law of gravitation, the weight of the object on the moon will be $W_m = G\frac{M_m \times m}{R_m^2}$ ... (a)<br>Let the weight of the same object on the earth be $W_e$. The mass of the earth is M and its radius is R. From eqs. $g = G\frac{M}{R^2}$ and $W = m \times g$<br>We have $W_e = G\frac{M \times m}{R^2}$ ... (b)<br>Substituting the values from Table 3.7 in Eqs. (a) and (b), we get<br>$W_m = G\frac{7.36 \times 10^{22}\,kg \times m}{(1.74 \times 10^6\,m)^2}$<br>$W_m = 2.431 \times 10^{10} G \times m$ (1)<br>and $W_e = 1.474 \times 10^{11} G \times m$ (2)<br>Dividing Eq. 1 by Eq. 2, we get<br>$\frac{W_m}{W_e} = \frac{2.431 \times 10^{10}}{1.474 \times 10^{11}}$<br>Or $\frac{W_m}{W_e} = 0.165 \approx \frac{1}{6}$ (3) | (iv) Students will note it down in their notebooks. |

| | |
|---|---|
| $\frac{\text{Weight of the object on the moon}}{\text{Weight of the object on the earth}} = \frac{1}{6}$ <br> weight of the object on the moon $= (1/6) \times$ its Weight on the earth. | |

(8) **Sample problems**

| Problems | Solutions |
|---|---|
| (i) If mass of an object is 10 kg, then what is its weight on the earth? | (i) Mass, m = 10 kg <br> Acceleration due to gravity, g = 9.8 $ms^{-2}$ <br> $W = m \times g$ <br> $W = 10 \text{ kg} \times 9.8 \text{ ms}^{-2} = 98 \text{ N}$ <br> Thus, the weight of the object is 98 N. |
| (ii) An object weighs 10 N when measured on the surface of the earth. What would be its weight when measured on the surface of the moon? | (ii) We know, <br> Weight of object on the moon = (1/6) × its weight on the earth. <br> That is, <br> $W_m = \frac{W_e}{6} = \frac{10}{6}$ N. <br> = 1.67 N. <br> Thus, the weight of object on the surface of the moon would be 1.67 N. |

(9) **Recapitulation**

- Why is the weight of an object on the moon $1/6^{th}$ its weight on the earth?
- What are the differences between the mass of an object and its weight?

(10) **Homework**

- What is the magnitude of the gravitational force between the earth and a 1 kg object on its surface? (Mass of the earth is $6 \times 10^{24}$ kg and radius of the earth is $6.4 \times 10^{6}$ m.)
- If mass of a person is 70 kg, then what is his weight on the earth?

# LESSON PLAN – 19

| | |
|---|---|
| **Subject:** Science | **Date:** ________ |
| **Topic:** Rate of doing work | **Duration:** 35 – 40 minutes |
| | **Class:** 10th |

**(1) General Objectives**

- To develop the interest of students in learning science.
- To develop the abilities of imagination, reasoning and observation.
- To inculcate creativity in students.
- To develop the understanding about the reality and observation.
- To enable them to get knowledge contained in the lesson.

**(2) Specific Objectives**

- To enable the students to learn about rate of doing work.
- To enable the students to learn about power and average power.
- To enable the students to learn about watt, W.

**(3) Previous Knowledge**

The students must have at least general familiarities with work, scientific conception of work, energy, forms of energy, i.e. kinetic energy, potential energy, potential energy of an object at a height, i.e. gravitational potential energy and law of conservation of energy.

**(4) Teaching Aids**

Blackboard, chalk, duster, pointer, models and other required materials.

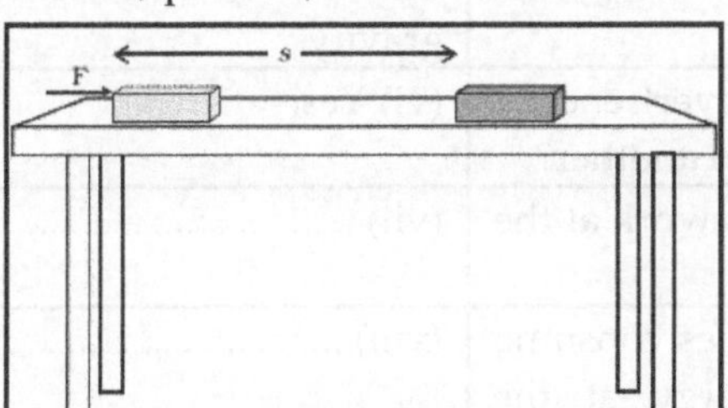


**Fig. 3.24**

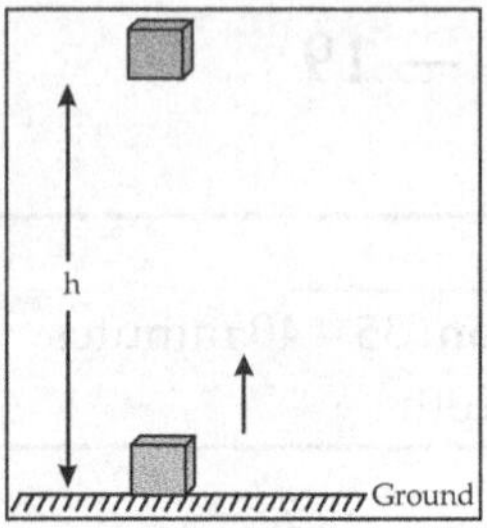


Fig. 3.25

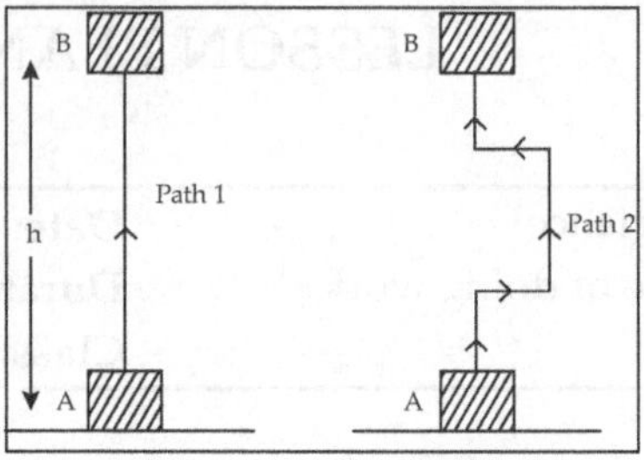


Fig. 3.26

## (5) Introduction

| Teacher's Question | Student's Answer |
|---|---|
| (i) What do you know about work? | (i) Work refers to an activity involving a force and movement in the direction of the force. |
| (ii) Good, now tell me about scientific conception of work. | (ii) We define work to be equal to the product of the force and displacement, thus,<br>Work done = force × displacement or<br>$W = F \times s$ |
| (iii) What do you know about energy? | (iii) Energy is the capacity of a physical system to perform work. |
| (iv) Good, tell me about kinetic energy or potential energy. | (iv) The kinetic energy of an object is the energy, which it possesses due to its motion. Potential energy is the energy of an object or a system due to the position of the body or the arrangement of the particles of the system. |
| (v) Very good, now tell me about potential energy of an object at a height (or gravitational potential energy). | (v) The gravitational potential energy of an object at a point above the ground is defined as the work done in raising it from the ground to that point against gravity. |
| (vi) Can we convert energy from one form to another? | (vi) Yes. |
| (vii) Do all of us work at the same rate? | (vii) .................................. |
| (viii) Do machines consume or transfer energy at the same rate? | (viii) .................................. |

**(6) Statement of topic**

Now, teacher will announce the topic, "Today, we will study about rate of doing work."

**(7) Presentation**

| Teacher's Action | Student's Activity |
|---|---|
| (i) Teacher will tell all the students that a stronger person may do certain work in relatively less time. A more powerful vehicle would complete a journey in a shorter time than a less powerful one. We talk of the power of machines like motorbikes and motorcars. The speed with which these vehicles change energy or do work is a basis for their classification. | (i) After listening teacher, students will note it down in their notebooks. |
| (ii) Teacher will tell that power measures the speed of work done, that is, how fast or slow work is done. Power is defined as the rate of doing work or the rate of transfer of energy. If an agent does a work W in time t, then power is given by:<br>Power = work/time or $P = W/t$ .... (b)<br>The unit of power is watt having the symbol W. One watt is the power of an agent, which does work at the rate of 1 joule per second. We can also say that power is 1 W when the rate of consumption of energy is $1\ J\ s^{-1}$.<br>1 watt = 1 joule/second or $1\ W = 1\ J\ s^{-1}$.<br>We express larger rates of energy transfer in kilowatts (kW).<br>1 kilowatt = 1000 watts<br>1 kW = 1000 W<br>$1\ kW = 1000\ J\ s^{-1}$.<br>The power of an agent may vary with time. This means that the agent may be doing work at different rates at different intervals of time. Therefore, the concept of average power is useful. We obtain | (ii) Students will note it down in their notebooks. |

| average power by dividing the total energy consumed by the total time taken. | |
|---|---|

**(8) Sample problems**

| Problems | Solutions |
|---|---|
| (i) Two girls, each of weight 400 N climb up a rope through a height of 8 m. We name one of the girls A and the other B. Girl A takes 20 s while B takes 50 s to accomplish this task. What is the power expended by each girl? | (i) Power expended by girl A:<br>Weight of the girl, mg = 400 N<br>Displacement (height), h = 8 m<br>Time taken, t = 20 s<br>From Eq. (b), Power, P = Work done/time taken<br>$=\frac{mgh}{t}$<br>$=\frac{400N \times 8m}{20s}$<br>$=160W.$<br>Power expended by girl B:<br>Weight of the girl, mg = 400 N<br>Displacement (height), h = 8 m<br>Time taken, t = 50 s<br>$\text{Power}(P)=\frac{mgh}{t}$<br>$=\frac{400N \times 8m}{50s}=64W.$<br>Power expended by girl A is 160 W.<br>Power expended by girl B is 64 W. |
| (ii) A boy of mass 50 kg runs up a staircase of 45 steps in 9 s. If the height of each step is 15 cm, find his power. Take g = 10 m $s^{-2}$. | (ii) Weight of the boy,<br>mg = 50 kg × 10 m $s^{-2}$ = 500 N<br>Height of the staircase, h = 45 × 15/100 m = 6.75 m<br>Time taken to climb, t = 9 s<br>From Eq. (b), power, P = Work done/time taken<br>$=\frac{mgh}{t}$<br>$=\frac{500N \times 6.75m}{9s}=375W.$<br>Power is 375 W. |

**(9) Recapitulation**

- What is power?
- Define 1 watt of power.
- A lamp consumes 1000 J of electrical energy in 10 s. What is its power?
- Define average power.

**(10) Homework**

- The potential energy of a freely falling object decreases progressively. Does this violate the law of conservation of energy? Why?
- What are the various energy transformations that occur when you are riding a bicycle?

**TELL ME AND I FORGET. TEACH ME AND I REMEMBER. INVOLVE ME AND I LEARN.**

**— Benjamin Franklin**

# LESSON PLAN – 20

| | |
|---|---|
| **Subject:** Science | **Date:** ________ |
| **Topic:** Transportation in plants | **Duration:** 35 – 40 minutes |
| | **Class:** 10th |

**(1) General Objectives**

- To develop the interest of students in learning science.
- To develop the abilities of imagination, reasoning and observation.
- To inculcate creativity in students.
- To develop the understanding about the reality and observation.
- To enable them to get knowledge contained in the lesson.

**(2) Specific Objectives**

- To enable the students to learn about transportation in plants.
- To enable the students to know about transport of water in plants.
- To enable the students to know about transport of food and other substances in plants.
- To enable the students to know about components of the transport system in highly organised plants.

**(3) Previous Knowledge**

The students must have at least general familiarities with life processes, nutrition, autotrophic nutrition, heterotrophic nutrition, how do organisms obtain their nutrition, nutrition in human beings, respiration, transportation in human beings, etc.

**(4) Teaching Aids**

Blackboard, chalk, duster, pointer, models and other required materials.

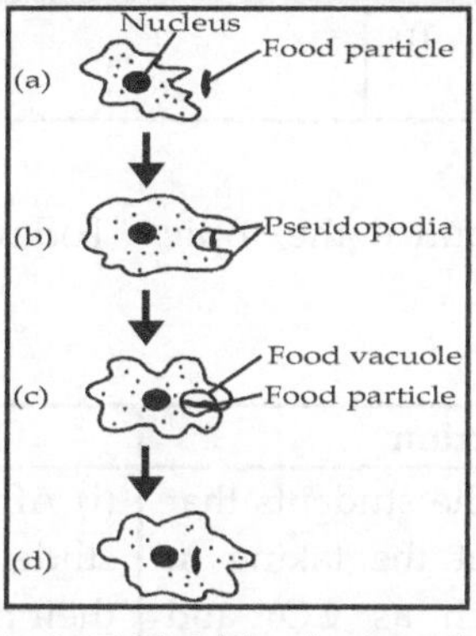


**Fig. 3.27: Nutrition in Amoeba**

## (5) Introduction

| Teacher's Question | Student's Answer |
|---|---|
| (i) What are life processes? | (i) The processes, which together perform the maintenance job, are life processes. |
| (ii) What do you know about nutrition? | (ii) Nutrition is the provision, to cells and organisms, of the materials necessary to support life. |
| (iii) How do living things get their food? | (iii) Some organisms use simple food material obtained from inorganic sources in the form of carbon dioxide and water. Other organisms utilise complex substances. |
| (iv) Good, explain auto-trophic nutrition. | (iv) The term autotrophic ('self-feeding') defines organisms, which are able to use external sources of energy in the synthesis of their organic food materials. |
| (v) What do you mean by heterotrophic nutrition? | (v) Heterotrophic ('other-feeding') organisms obtain their energy by breaking down substances obtained from the bodies of other organisms. |
| (vi) Very good, now tell me about respiration. | (vi) The process by which organisms exchange gases, especially oxygen and carbon dioxide, with the environment is called respiration. |
| (vii) Do you know about transportation in plants? | (vii) ........................................ |
| (xi) How are water and | (xi) ........................................ |

| minerals transported in plants? | |
|---|---|

**(6) Statement of topic**

Now, teacher will announce the topic, "Today, we will study about transportation in plants."

**(7) Presentation**

| Teacher's Action | Student's Activity |
|---|---|
| (i) Teacher will tell all the students that we already know about the taking in simple compounds such as $CO_2$ and photosynthesise energy stored in their chlorophyll-containing organs, namely leaves in plants. The other kinds of raw materials needed for building plant bodies will also have to be taken up separately. For plants, the soil is the nearest and richest source of raw materials like nitrogen, phosphorus and other minerals. The absorption of these substances therefore occurs through the part in contact with the soil, namely roots. If the distances between soil-contacting organs and chlorophyll-containing organs are small, energy and raw materials can easily diffuse to all parts of the plant body. But if these distances become large because of changes in plant body design, diffusion processes will not be sufficient to provide raw material in leaves and energy in roots. A proper system of transportation is therefore essential in such situations. | (i) After listening the teacher, students will note it down in their notebooks. |
| (ii) Teacher will tell that different amount of energy is needed by different body designs or structures.<br>Plants do not move and plant bodies have a large proportion of dead cells in many tissues. As a result, plants have | (ii) Students will note it down in their notebooks.<br>Some students ask about transportation of water and minerals in plants. |

| | |
|---|---|
| low energy needs and can use relatively slow transport systems. The distances over which transport systems have to operate, however, can be very large in plants such as very tall trees. Plant transport systems will move energy stores from leaves and raw materials from roots. These two pathways are constructed as independently organised conducting tubes. One, the xylem moves water and minerals obtained from the soil. The other, phloem transports products of photosynthesis from the leaves where they are synthesised to other parts of the plant. | |
| (iii) Teacher will tell that in xylem tissue, vessels and tracheids of the roots, stems and leaves are interconnected to form a continuous system of water-conducting channels reaching all parts of the plant. At the roots, cells in contact with the soil actively take up ions. This creates a difference in the concentration of these ions between the root and the soil. Water, therefore, moves into the root from the soil to eliminate this difference. This means that there is steady movement of water into root xylem, creating a column of water that is steadily pushed upwards. However, this pressure by itself is unlikely to be enough to move water over the heights that we commonly see in plants. Plants use another strategy to move water in the xylem upwards to the highest points of the plant body. | (iii) Students will note it down in their notebooks. |
| (iv) Teacher will tell provided (the plant has an adequate supply of water) that the water which is lost through the stomata is replaced by water from the | (iv) Students will note it down in their notebooks. |

| | |
|---|---|
| xylem vessels in the leaf. In fact, evaporation of water molecules from the cells of a leaf creates a suction, which pulls water from the xylem cells of roots. The loss of water in the form of vapour from the aerial parts of the plant is known as transpiration. | |
| (v) Teacher will tell thus, transpiration helps in the absorption and upward movement of water and minerals dissolved in it from roots to the leaves. It also helps in temperature regulation. The effect of root pressure in transport of water is more important at night. During the day when the stomata are open, the transpiration pull becomes the major driving force in the movement of water in the xylem. | (v) Students will note it down in their notebooks. Some students ask that how is food transported in plants. |
| (vi) Teacher will say, now let us consider how the products of metabolic processes, particularly photosynthesis, are moved from leaves, where they are formed, to other parts of the plant. This transport of soluble products of photosynthesis is called translocation and it occurs in the part of the vascular tissue known as phloem. Besides the products of photosynthesis, the phloem transports amino acids and other substances. These substances are especially delivered to the storage organs of roots, fruits, seeds and to growing organs. The translocation of food and other substances takes place in the sieve tubes with the help of adjacent companion cells both in upward and downward directions. Unlike transport in xylem, which can be largely explained by simple physical forces, the translocation in phloem is achieved by utilising energy. Material like sucrose is | (vi) Students will note it down in their notebooks. |

| | |
|---|---|
| transferred into phloem tissue using energy from ATP. This increases the osmotic pressure of the tissue causing water to move into it. This pressure moves the material in the phloem to tissues, which have less pressure. This allows the phloem to move material according to the plant's needs. For example, in the spring, sugar stored in root or stem tissue would be transported to the buds, which need energy to grow. | |

**(8) Experiment**

| Activity | Discussion | Result |
|---|---|---|
| Take two small pots of approximately the same size and having the same amount of soil. One should have a plant in it. Place a stick of the same height as the plant in the other pot.<br>Cover the soil in both pots with a plastic sheet so that moisture cannot escape by evaporation.<br>Cover both sets, one with the plant and the other with the stick, with plastic sheets and place in bright sunlight for half an hour. | Do you observe any difference in the two cases? | We will find water droplets collected on the inner side of the plastic sheet of pot containing a plant. This shows that the process of transportation occurs in plants. |

**(9) Recapitulation**

- What are the components of the transport system in highly organised plants?
- How are water and minerals transported in plants?
- How is food transported in plants?

**(10) Homework**

(a) The autotrophic mode of nutrition requires

(i) carbon dioxide and water

(ii) chlorophyll

(iii) sunlight

(iv) all of the above

(b) The breakdown of pyruvate to give carbon dioxide, water and energy takes place in:

(i) cytoplasm

(ii) mitochondria

(iii) chloroplast

(iv) nucleus

(c) What are the differences between the transport of materials in xylem and phloem?

**TEACHERS OPEN THE DOOR. YOU ENTER BY YOURSELF**

**— Chinese proverb**

*"We cannot hold a torch to light another's path without brightenin our own.."*

*– Ben Swwetland*

# 4 Microteaching

The quality of education that is provided to our children depends on the quality of our teachers. The quality of teachers, in turn, definitely depends on the way in which they had received training through teacher's training institutions. The question that immediately arises now is about the teacher education programme. Hence, we must take a peep into this programme. The need of planning is essential. If our teachers are going to shape the destiny of our country, teacher education has to assume a great responsibility and has to take recourse to some innovative and effective technique of training teachers. It was believed that just as the director brings the skill of giving life and form to a movie, so the teacher brings to the teaching-learning situation the skill with which he/she is able to control and use his/her teaching exercise and thus influence the other variables of the situation. This skill does not automatically come to the teacher with a certificate or diploma or a teaching contract. Rather, it is a skill developed through the awareness of the interacting elements in a teaching-learning situation, planning strategies for teaching based on this awareness, through the setting of sound objectives, assessing the results and modifying these objectives in terms of assessment. In India, the education system made for the traditional teacher education programme consisted of two major parts:

- Theoretical Course, and
- Practice teaching.

The theoretical course, which covers philosophical, historical, sociological and psychological foundation of education and teaching methodology, is mainly verbal, abstract and vague. Consequently, it affects cognitive and attitudinal rather than behavioural changes in teachers. With regard to practice teaching, it is assumed that during this period, the pupil teacher will develop proficiency in basic teaching skills and classroom management. In actual practice, however, the programme of student teaching tends to him theoretical and lacks the objective feedback on performance, essential to both motivating and directing behavioural modifications. Hence, improvements were felt to the required not only in the theoretical aspect of the teacher-education curriculum, but also in the application of teaching skills.

## Definition of Microteaching

Microteaching is a procedure in which a pupil teacher practice teaching with a reduced number of pupils in a reduced period of time with emphasis on a narrow and specific teaching skill. Thus, microteaching is a scaled-down encounter in class size and class time. It is, therefore a skill based approach to teacher training. Microteaching is a technique of presenting a small portion of the lesson for detailed study and pinpointed guidance by taking a microscopic view. Reducing the number of students in the class, the duration of the lesson, the portion of the content and the number of skills to be practiced minimises the complexities of the usual classroom teaching.

Thus, microteaching is a training technique, which requires pupil teachers to teach a single concept, using specified teaching skills to a small number of pupils in a short duration of time. Microteaching is a training technique and the idea underlying this technique is that the teaching act consists of different skills. Each skill can be developed separately through training. The basic contention is that, more the number of skills in which a person is trained, the more efficient he/she will be as a teacher.

Accordingly, this technique is mainly for developing certain skills of teaching procedure, which contains the following steps:

- Modeling the skill.
- Planning a micro lesson.
- The teaching session.

- The critique session.
- The re-planning session.
- The re-teach session.
- The re-critique session.

**(1) Modeling the skill**

It is essential to orient the trainees in the teaching skill to be practiced. This may be done though stating the psychological base and rationale of the skill and then demonstrating the said skill. This step is called Modeling. Models are of two types:

- **Perceptual Model:** Perceptual model is one, which is presented by way of demonstration and is visually perceived by the trainee.
- **Conceptual Model:** The conceptual model is usually presented in the form of written material and is conceptualised by trainees.

  The microteaching technique usually uses the perceptual model, which enables the trainees of focus their attention on the skill to be practiced and to perceive the pinpointed behaviour.

**(2) Planning a Micro lesson**

It is necessary to select an appropriate content, which yields maximum scope for practicing the skill. A lesson of a short duration, usually of 5 to 7 minutes, is then planned in consultation with the supervisor. With these two steps, namely, modeling and lesson planning, the stage is set for safe practice teaching.

**(3) The teaching Session**

The plan of the lesson is now executed in the presence of the supervisor and/or peer trainees. The performance of a micro teacher is observed in relation to the skills to be acquired and is recorded. An evaluation sheet tape recorder, video tapes all of these or either of these evaluation tools is used for this purpose.

**(4) The Critique Session**

The students leave the class and the supervisor and/or the peer group discusses the micro teacher's performance. Trainees' concrete and pinpointed feedback is then given in 5 to 7 minutes for the specific improvement. The evaluation tools (videotape, etc.) give a rare opportunity to the micro teacher to view his/her performance objectively. They hardly give him/her an opportunity to put forth self-defence. This is a strong point of the microteaching technique.

**(5) The Re-Planning Session**

The micro-teacher recognises this each teaching plan on the basis of the feedback offered in the critique session. Usually, 5 to 7 minutes are allotted to this.

**(6) The Re-Teaching Session**

This step provides the micro teacher an opportunity to teach the same unit. The re-planning session is followed by the re-teaching session, which runs for 5 to 7 minutes. The same unit is taught to another batch of 5 to 7 pupils. The supervisor and/or the peer trainee observer evaluate the performance of the micro teacher with the evaluation tools. This step provides the micro teacher an opportunity to teach the same unit without considering time lag.

**(7) The Re-Critique Session**

The same procedure is adopted as mentioned in the critique session. The micro teacher again gets the feedback and knows the extent of his/her improvement. If handled properly, this step has the potential to motivate the micro teacher to improve his/her performance.

**(8) The Seven Steps in Microteaching**

The microteaching has seven important steps without which we cannot complete the process. These steps are as follows:

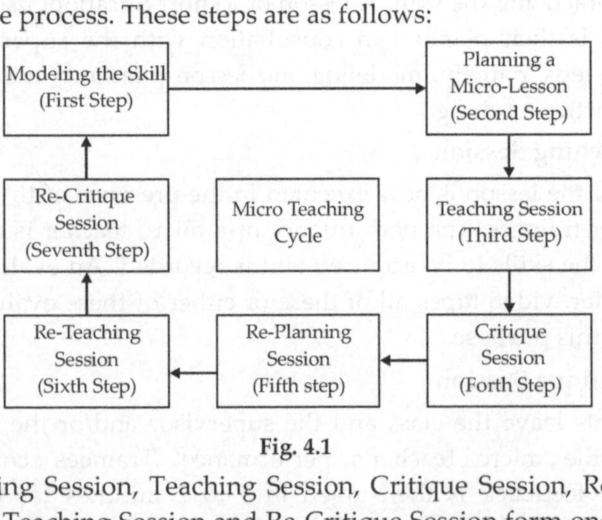


**Fig. 4.1**

Planning Session, Teaching Session, Critique Session, Re-Planning Session, Re-Teaching Session and Re-Critique Session form one complete cycle of microteaching procedure. This cycle may be repeated according to the necessity of improvement. The entire procedure for a micro lesson then runs as follows:

First of all, there is a theoretical discussion on a particular skill to be practiced. Its components are defined in precise terms. This is followed by demonstration and modeling. The student teachers observe the particular skill. After this, a suitable unit is chosen and the student teacher prepares a lesson plan and gets ready for a micro lesson. The lesson is taught and criticised by the peer group. As per criticism/feedback, the student teacher plans his/her lesson again and it goes on.

Microteaching is thus mainly concerned with acquiring the teaching skills. It is thus the planned interaction between the teacher and the taught. Now, it is not possible to go to schools and practice this skill, as the principals of the schools will never like the idea of allowing only 5 to 7 pupils at a time. This will disturb their schedule too. So, to overcome this problem, the student teachers are asked to give lessons to their own peer group. This is called "Simulation".

## Positive Aspects of Microteaching

- There comes a major awareness to pupil teachers with regard to professional training.
- There is more scope for practice in teaching skills according to the student's potential.
- It develops confidence by having the practice of skills in microteaching under simulated conditions.
- It creates more general teaching competence among the pupil-teachers.
- It allows for different strategies for supervisory feedback.
- Micro-teaching helps to identify categories in which additional research is needed.
- Micro-teaching helps in improving the methods of criticising student's performance.
- It determines the length of training time required to master certain skills.
- Micro-teaching helps in improving the ways of analysing pupil learning.

- Micro-teaching focuses attention on teacher behaviour.
- It offers opportunity to practice a real lesson without the complexities of a normal classroom (great advantage of working under simulated conditions).
- If offers several sources of immediate feedback.
- One skill is learnt at a time.
- It equips the beginner with an array of teaching skills before he/she faces the real classroom situation.
- Evaluation procedure of a micro lesson is more precise, objective and acceptable.
- Major steps of a micro lesson are towards individualising the training of teachers.
- It helps in the development of self-confidence.
- It helps in being acquainted with classroom manners to a certain extent.
- It helps the trainees to develop the skill of blackboard writing.
- It is helpful in improving his/her own teaching.

## Practicing Skills of Questioning in Microteaching

The skill of asking questions in the classroom teaching is very important. By asking questions again and again, the teacher makes the pupils more thoughtful. He/she enables them to understand and subjects deeply. Questions are those, which help the pupils to think in depth about the various aspects of the problem. The teacher can use the questions in the following situations:

**(1) Prompting:** Prompting is the situation, which arises when a pupil expresses his inability to answer some questions in the class or his answer is incomplete. The teacher can ask such questions, which prompt the pupils in solving the already asked questions.

**(2) Seeking further Information:** In class, when the pupils are unable to answer any question or answer partially, then in order to receive complete and correct answer, the teacher can ask such questions by accepting that the answer given is correct, but the pupil should reveal more. There can be alternate answer to the question asked such as elaborate the answer more. In this way, the teacher can seek maximum information from the pupils.

**(3) Refocusing:** Sometimes, the teacher may ask probing questions to concentrate the attention of the pupils. For the very same purpose, the teacher may ask same question from other pupil. This is known as 'Refocusing.'

**(4) Redirection:** If the teacher wants to introduce the pupils with various aspects of the problem in classroom then he can ask the same question after slight changes in the language. This technique is known as 'Redirection'.

**(5) Critical Awareness:** In order to develop the reasoning power of the pupils in class, the teacher can ask questions bearing 'Why', by getting motivate from such questions, pupils involve themselves in the process of reasoning. This is known as 'Critical Awareness' technique.

**Table 4.1**

| Components | Rating scale |
|---|---|
| Prompting | 1 |
| Seeking further information | 2 |
| Refocusing | 3 |
| Redirection | 4 |
| Increasing critical awareness | 5 |

# Special Care to Our Students!

Get

**'How to pass IGNOU Exams' Book**

Worth Rs.199/-

# FREE

Register now on Gullybaba and download book from download section.

↓

https://bit.ly/HowtoPassIGNOUExam

*"Education is the best provision for the journey to old age."*

*– Aristotle*

# 5 Lesson Planning based on Microteaching

## LESSON PLAN – 1

| **Subject:** Science | **Date:** ______ |
|---|---|
| **Topic:** Balanced diet | **Duration:** 10 minutes |
| | **Class:** 6th |

| S.No. | Teacher's action | Student's Activity | Component Rating Scale |
|---|---|---|---|
| (i) | Students, do you know about nutrients? | Yes, substances provide nourishment essential for growth and the maintenance of life. | 1, 2 and 3 |
| (ii) | Well, tell me about balanced diet. | .......................... | 2 and 4 |
| (iii) | The food we normally eat in a day is our diet. For growth and main-tenance of good health, our diet should have all the nutrients that our body needs, in right quantities is a balanced diet. Not too much of one and not too little of the other. The | Students will note it down in their note-books. | 1, 3, 4 and 5 |

| | | | |
|---|---|---|---|
| | balanced diet also contains a good amount of roughage and water. | | |
| (iv) | Pulses, groundnut, soya bean, sprouted seeds (moong and Bengal gram), fermented foods (South Indian foods such as idlis), a com-bination of flours (missi roti, thepla made from cereals and pulses), banana, spinach, sattu, jaggery, available vege-tables and other such foods provide many nutrients. Therefore, one can eat a balanced diet without expensive food materials. | Students will note it down in their note-books. | 1, 3, 4 and 5 |
| (v) | Eating the right kind of food is not enough. It should also be cooked properly so that its nutrients are not lost. | Students will note it down in their note-books. | 1, 3, 4 and 5 |
| (vi) | Are you aware that some nutrients get lost in the process of cooking and preparations? | ............................ | 2 and 4 |
| (vii) | If the vegetables and fruits are washed after cutting or peeling them, it may result in the loss of some vitamins. The skins of many vege-tables and fruits contain vitamins and minerals. Similarly, repeated wash-ing of rice and pulses may remove some vitamins and minerals present in them. | Students will note it down in their note-books. | 1, 3, 4 and 5 |

# LESSON PLAN – 2

| **Subject:** Science | **Date:** ________ |
|---|---|
| **Topic:** Blood | **Duration:** 10 minutes |
| | **Class:** 7th |

| S.No. | Teacher's action | Student's Activity | Component Rating Scale |
|---|---|---|---|
| (i) | Students, you know that organisms need food, water and oxygen for survival. They need to transport all these to various parts of their body. Further, animals need to transport wastes to parts from where they can be removed. Have you wondered how all this is achieved? | .............................. | 2 and 4 |
| (ii) | Ok, what happens when you get a cut on your body? | Blood flows out | 1, 2 and 3 |
| (iii) | Good, but what is blood? | .............................. | 2 and 4 |
| (iv) | Blood is the fluid, which flows in blood vessels. It transports substances like digested food from the small intestine to the other parts of the body. It carries oxygen from the lungs to the cells of the body. It also transports waste for removal from the body. | Students will note it down in their notebooks. Students ask how the blood carries various substances. | 1, 3, 4 and 5 |
| (v) | Blood is a liquid, which has cells of various kinds suspended in it. | Students will note it down in their notebooks. Students ask for the reason of the red colour of the blood. | 1, 3, 4 and 5 |
| (vi) | The fluid part of the blood | Students will note it | 1, 3, 4 and 5 |

| | | | |
|---|---|---|---|
| | is called plasma. One type of cells is the red blood cells (RBC) which contains a red pigment called hemoglobin. Hemoglobin bind with oxygen and transports it to all the parts of the body and ultimately to all the cells. It will be difficult to provide oxygen efficiently to all the cells of the body without hemoglobin. The presence of hemoglobin makes blood appear red. | down in their note-books. | |

**TEACHER APPRECIATION MAKES THE WORLD OF EDUCATION GO AROUND.**

— **Helen Peters**

# LESSON PLAN — 3

| **Subject:** Science | **Date:** ________ |
|---|---|
| **Topic:** Natural Resources | **Duration:** 10 minutes |
| | **Class:** 8th |

| S.No. | Teacher's action | Student's Activity | Component Rating Scale |
|---|---|---|---|
| (i) | Students, we use various materials for our basic needs. Some of them are found in nature and some have been made by human efforts. Does this list include air, water, soil and minerals? | Yes, the list includes air, water, soil and minerals. | 1, 2 and 3 |
| (ii) | Since all these are obtained from nature, they are called natural resources. | Ok, can we use all our natural resources forever? | 1, 2 and 3 |
| (iii) | In the light of the availability of various resources in nature, natural resources can be broadly classified into two kinds: *Inexhaustible Natural Resources:* These resources are present in unlimited quantity in nature and are not likely to be exhausted by human activities. Examples are sunlight and air. *Exhaustible Natural Resources:* The amount of these resources in nature is limited. They | Students will note it down in their note-books. | 1, 3, 4 and 5 |

| | | | |
|---|---|---|---|
| | can be exhausted by human activities. Examples of these resources are forests, wildlife, minerals, coal, petroleum, natural gas, etc. | | |
| (iv) | Some exhaustible natural resources like coal, petroleum and natural gas are formed from the dead remains of living organisms (fossils). So, these are all known as fossil fuels. | Students will note it down in their notebooks. | 1, 3, 4 and 5 |

**COME FORTH INTO THE LIGHT OF THINGS, LET NATURE BE YOUR TEACHER.**

**— William Wordsworth**

# LESSON PLAN – 4

| **Subject:** Science | **Date:** ________ |
|---|---|
| **Topic:** Tissue | **Duration:** 10 minutes |
| | **Class: 9th** |

| S.No. | Teacher's Action | Student's Activity | Component Rating Scale |
|---|---|---|---|
| (i) | Students, do you know about tissues? | Yes, a group of cells that are similar in structure and/or work together to achieve a particular function forms a tissue. | 2 and 3 |
| (ii) | Good, are plants and animals made of same types of tissues? | ................................ | 2 and 4 |
| (iii) | There are noticeable differences between the two. Plants are stationary or fixed they don't move. Most of the tissues they have are supportive, which provides them with structural strength. Most of these tissues are dead, since dead cells can provide mechanical strength as easily as live ones and need less maintenance. | Students will note it down in their notebooks and some students ask about animal tissues. | 1, 3, 4 and 5 |
| (iv) | Animals on the other hand move around in search of food, mates and shelter. They consume more energy as compared to plants. Most of the tissues they contain are living. | Students will note it down in their notebooks. | 1, 3, 4 and 5 |
| (v) | Another difference between animals and plants is in the | Students will note it down in their | 1, 3, 4 and 5 |

| | | | |
|---|---|---|---|
| | pattern of growth. The growth in plants is limited to certain regions, while this is not so in animals. There are some tissues in plants that divide throughout their life. These tissues are localised in certain regions. Based on the dividing capacity of the tissues, various plant tissues can be classified as growing or meristematic tissue and permanent tissue. | notebooks. | |

**TEACHNOLOGY IS JUST A TOOL. IN TERMS OF GETTING THE KIDS WORKING TOGETHER AND MOTIVATING THEM, THE TEACHER IS THE MOST IMPORTANT**

**— Bill Gates**

*"Real learning comes about when the competitive spirit has ceased."*

*– Jiddu Krishnamurti*

# 6 Become an Ideal Pedagogue

## Definition of a Good Teacher

An American definition of 'Teaching' envisages that 'Teaching is the consistent and effective transfer of appropriate behaviours which lead to the achievement of pre-determined and specified results'. Hence, in order to substantiate the purpose of teaching that is the transfer of knowledge to the students properly so that after receiving teachings they can acquire expected knowledge and pre-determined results. Thus, a good teacher is s/he who teaches the students how to lead their lives cleanly and controlled towards acquiring knowledge. The quality of a good teacher is vitality important for ideal teachings to the students. S/he should know the correct way of teaching where the students are inspired to learn and devote themselves to study.

"A good teacher is a facilitator of learning, one who gives out the information and explains things. It's someone who sees students as a whole person, and tries to address the whole child. They have high expectations, but also compassion."

***– Hana Ahmad, fifth-grade teacher at Orangewood Elementary in Fort Myers and a 2001 Golden Apple award winner.***

Some other important definitions of a teacher are:

- An effective teacher is a good person who meets the community ideal for a good citizen, good parent, and good employee. S/he is expected to be honest, hardworking, generous, friendly, and considerate, and to demonstrate these qualities in their classrooms by being authoritative, organized, disciplined, insightful, and dedicated. However, this definition lacks clear objective standards of performance.

- An effective teacher is one who concerns students' learning outcomes. S/he is expected to demonstrate five key behaviors and five helping behaviors in teaching. Five key behaviors are: (a) lesson clarity, (b) instructional variety, (c) task orientation, (d) engagement in the learning process, and (e) student success. Five helping behaviors are: (a) using student ideas and contributions, (b) structuring, (c) questioning, (d) probing, and (e) teacher affect.
- An effective teacher is one who has an achievement-motivated personality with a strong commitment and rich teaching experiences. S/he is expected to has a motivation to teach, empathy towards children, and good records at college GPA and student teaching.

  However, this definition does not reflect a teacher's day-to-day work in the classroom, does not include the most important and obvious measure of all for determining good teaching: the performance of the students who are being taught.

## What should you do being a good teacher?

According to Comonenius, a famous educationist, in order to make teaching successful, the three things are vitally important, i.e. good teachers, good methods and good books. Indeed, good teachers play a vital role in making teachings to the students successful. Being a teacher, s/he should behave in such a way by dint of his/her own image, voice and body use so that interaction and transfer of behaviour between the teacher and the students are accelerated in a systematic manner.

About the image, s/he needs to behave in the following manner:

- S/he should be well dressed and well rested.
- S/he has to arrive before the students and greet the students as they arrive.
- S/he needs to be enthusiastic about teaching in relevant field.

- S/he has to identify and help the students who are with problems or weak in studies.
- S/he should remain alert and concentrate on how his/her students are behaving.
- S/he should be an attentive, calm and quiet listener as well as speaker.

## Voice and Body Language used by a Good Teacher

In order to make our teachings memorable by good preparation, the teacher should use an effective voice. Besides this, s/he should have the following characteristics regarding voice:

- A teacher must start and end with bang.
- In between check and interaction, a teacher should understand one thing that the students are learning.
- To plan for accurate timing
- To choose suitable teaching methods in respect of the students and topics with a great care. In addition, s/he should help the students in learning, especially those who are with problems.

Apropos to the use of voice, one who will be a good teacher must be well conversant with the following:

- Are you audible to the students at the back?
- Whether you create excitedly enthusiasm?
- Quickly to stimulate?
- Are you enthusiastically able to stop boredom?
- Are you using good examples to highlight important points?
- Are you sounding confident and able to control the class?

An ideal teacher needs to play a vital role in active advisor among the students. S/he needs to be careful about the criteria as follows:

- *Control:* To draw up and issue instruction and stay with the students, closely supervising its action.
- *Guide:* To clarify what is required, hand over ownership to students and offer to give advice when they call you.

- *Consult*: To give a broad outline, ask students to discuss ideas and agree actions, using us as a separate expert reference point.
- *Facilitate:* To give overall direction, co-ordinate the group's discussion and expect it to produce a progress report.

A teacher's attitude may vary according to the nature of the students' subject area. Being a teacher, s/he needs to be very careful in using his/her voice for effective teaching class. A good teacher needs not to be excited and agitated towards the students. S/hee should give chance to ask question to the students so that transfer of behaviour is made possible in a significant manner. Sometimes, s/he forgets that a teacher has a particular job for the students on the concept of learning. According to Franchise Bacon, there are two types of learning: One is 'Pedagogy', i.e. children learning and the other is 'Andragogy', i.e. adult learning. In case of adult learning, teacher cannot teach anybody, s/he only helps him or her to learn. So, in the case of using voice, a teacher needs to be responsible and tactful. Hence, Somerset Maugham says, "It is difficult to pass over the razor's edge, but the wise say the path to salvation is hard".

A teacher should be careful in using his/her body. In this connection, s/he should bear in mind the following points:

- To think of the image, teacher wants to convey and practice and how shall s/he achieve it?
- Is s/he neatly/comfortably dressed?
- Shall s/he fidget with a pen, watch, glasses, etc.?
- Shall s/he makes eye contact?
- Shall s/he sit or s/he stand?

That is to say, a teacher's behaviour will be in such a manner that must attract the students for effective and efficient teaching.

## Lecturing the Students

In delivering lecture, there are limitations, which may create hindrance in learning on the part of the students. Sometimes the lecture may be monotonous and boring due to continuous saying. If there exists dryness amongst the students, the teacher should change the policy of his/her lecture. S/he should ask open-ended questions. Open-ended questions help in getting the students involved. Assuming to know a particular thing, students may get interested if s/he is intended to know those particular items. Some of the limitations of delivering a lecture are as follows:

- Not to ask open-ended questions to get students involved.
- To use agitated words.
- Not to repeat while delivering lecture.
- Not to ask meaningful questions.
- To ask several questions at a time.
- Not to give feedback on answers yourself or involve others.
- Not to give people a chance to absorb the question and answer it.
- Not to welcome answers.
- To be critical in answering and asking questions.

An ideal teacher needs to be well conversant about using the language. It is indispensable to create awareness and congenial atmosphere on the part of a teacher. The following are the different ways to improve lecture:

- To manage intersperse lecture with opportunities to challenge and discuss what is being delivered.
- To break the students into groups for exercises, which develop lecture themes and need to be reported back and analysed.
- To use case studies, which challenge students to apply the teaching, they are being given.
- To use video record teaching sessions and analyse progress and results.
- To use role-plays to demonstrate examples of what is said in lectures.
- To split into teams that analyse the days lecture theme and give a resume of it on same/next day.
- To be prepared to facilitate and contribute to discussions and help groups prepare feedback.
- To develop feedback techniques on what a teacher observes groups doing.

In order to develop lecture, group discussion is a vital thing. As a teacher, we have to ensure that group performance is effective.

From the students' point of view, a good teacher needs to inform the following rules of Franchise Bacon:

- Be on time.
- Be obedient.
- Be courteous.
- Wait for the turn of the students
- No visitors during classes/messages on notice board.
- Stay in your seat, be with the class.
- Be attentive.
- Contribute to what is happening.
- We are a team here - be a team layer.
- To be particular in doing home-task and taking part in active role on social and cultural affairs of the students.

Apropos to the teaching method, the following are important to apply in teaching the students virtually:

- Telling is not teaching
- Age is not a bar to learn
- Meaningful learning experience
- Voice, image and body use
- Practically oriented way of teaching
- Repeat, Recap and Review

In view of the above, a good teacher selects any method to teach the students but according to Franchise Bacon, most of the good teachers select the sixth rule of teaching, i.e. 'Repeat, Recap and Review' which is the most important one to make the teaching vitally effective, meaningful, fruitful and up to the mark.

The reasons in support of the argument are stated as follows:

**Repeat**

According to Franchise Bacon, 'when you tell something in the class to a group of students, it is only a saying but when you recapitulate it, repeat it and ask the question on the progress, it will be interacted and if you further emphasise the concept, they will be conversant with the relevant knowledge'. Indeed, in case of delivering an important message, if it is stated once-only 10 per cent will be memorised but if it is stated 6 times, then 90 per cent will be memorised after one year. So, reiteration /repetition is the most important tool for the teaching to make the topics rememberable. If the message is not remembered and understandable then the whole thing will be treated as useless.

**Recap**

It is generally meant by recap to go over again the vital point of the relevant contents. Using FULLR and VHF for better memorisation can do the recap. As the first events are best-memorised so to start with big message, thereafter, use unusual event like cartoon, exercise, etc. Thirdly, linked event, here mnemonics or analogy can be used and lastly to end with big messages of fascination towards the topics. In this context, summing up the ideas to arrive the conclusion that is the gist in question to be communicated to the students as a good communicator of the teaching course. According to Commoneus, for an effective teaching, 'only lecture is immaterial but in order to ornament it for better memorisation, ideal approach, demonstration, visual display and varieties of attractions of the students are needed'.

**Review**

'To err is human' means that it is human nature to forget the things/message, which is not reviewed that are a teacher losing what s/he don't review. To review the important messages, teachers have to regularly sum up where they have reached and invited questions.

At the end of every topics if the teacher repeats, recap and review, ask questions and help them to answer properly, the trainees will be more motivated and conversant with the subjects and grasp it properly so that teaching will be effective and fruitful.

Gullybaba.com

SCHOLARSHIP

We Care for You!

यदि आप Corona की वजह से IGNOU की फीस का इंतजाम नहीं कर पा रहे हैं तो नीचे दिए गए मोबाइल फोन पर संपर्क करें।

Call or Whatsapp. 9212232302